Group Interventions in Schools

Elaine Clanton Harpine

Group Interventions
in Schools

Promoting Mental Health for At-Risk
Children and Youth

 Springer

Elaine Clanton Harpine
University of South California
Aiken, SC
USA
clantonharpine@hotmail.com

ISBN: 978-0-387-77315-5   e-ISBN: 978-0-387-77317-9
DOI: 10.1007/978-0-387-77317-9

Library of Congress Control Number: 2008920065

Printed on acid-free paper

9 8 7 6 5 4 3 2 1

springer.com

To my loving husband, Bill, for his never-ending support and encouragement.

Preface

This book, which is intended for psychologists, school counselors, and school-based health practitioners, discusses the theoretical structure of group interventions in schools, and gives examples of how to use these interventions. Although there are many forms of group interventions in school-based settings, this book concentrates on group-centered interventions, which are prevention-oriented group programs that enable students with academic-based problems to learn to function more successfully.

Group-centered interventions focus on helping students develop cognitive, affective, and behavioral skills through structured, hands-on group sessions. An element of play is added for children, and programs for adolescents incorporate service to the community. As the term *group-centered* implies, all interventions discussed in this book use the therapeutic power of groups. If properly harnessed, group cohesion can be a powerful agency for change.

This book is written for those who wish to learn how to use group-centered interventions in school-based settings. School-based settings offer opportunities not only during school hours, but also before school and after school, and includes community-related programs for schoolchildren.

For school counselors who have limited training in designing and facilitating group interventions with children, this book can serve either as a training manual or as supplemental reading. It can also help group specialists who wish to fine-tune their skills, and beginning practitioners who have little group experience. By the end of this book, the reader will know how to use group-centered interventions in a school-based setting.

It is difficult to understand how to use groups by simply reading case studies or theory. Find a group to observe or work with as you read. Putting concepts into a real-world setting brings theory to life.

Each chapter begins with a case study from a group-centered intervention in a school-based situation, and ends with an observational exercise and a ready-to-use group intervention that reinforces the chapter's theoretical principles. Chapters 1 through 4 outline the theoretical structure of group-centered interventions. Chapter 5 looks at the advantages and disadvantages of using group interventions. Chapter 6 gives a detailed look at how to use a group-centered intervention in a school-based setting. Chapters 7 and 8 discuss applying, selecting, and designing a group-centered intervention to meet school-based needs. Chapter 9 outlines how to evaluate the effectiveness of your group intervention program. I hope that this book will energize the reader's creative skills and excite the desire to use group-centered interventions.

Working with children and adolescents takes patience, and, most of all, the desire to help young people reach their full potential in life. Young people desperately want to belong, to be accepted. They spend much of their lives in school or with school groups; while they are there, we have the chance not only to educate them but also to help them improve their lives. If we fail to meet their needs today, we will most likely not have another chance tomorrow. Group-centered interventions can help us chart a pathway that will help today's children and adolescents find a brighter tomorrow.

Aiken, SC   Elaine Clanton Harpine

Acknowledgments

I wish to express my appreciation to Judy Jones, my editor, for her support and help in the development of this book. I also want to thank my husband for his love and support throughout the project, and for his patience and helpful comments on the text. I would also like to thank my three children, David, Virginia, and Christina, who have all worked as reading tutors in my Camp Sharigan program over the years. A thank you also goes to all of the children, adolescents, and university students who I have had the pleasure of working with while developing group-centered interventions.

Contents

About the Author

Elaine Clanton Harpine, Ph.D., is a motivational psychologist specializing in group-centered motivational program design. She has 35 years' experience designing and conducting motivational programs for children and adolescents. Dr. Clanton Harpine earned her doctorate in educational psychology and counseling from the University of Illinois–Urbana-Champaign.

Dr. Clanton Harpine has published eight nonfiction books, including *No Experience Necessary!,* which received an Award of Excellence in 1995 and was selected as one of the top five children's books in its class. Other published children's writings include a two-volume series entitled, *Come Follow Me,* in 2001; a three-volume family series completed in 2003; a book for adolescents in 1989, along with numerous articles for teenagers on peer pressure, coping with failure, alcohol abuse, parents, and suicide; and more recently, articles on using group-centered interventions in the schools.

Dr. Clanton Harpine has been interviewed on local early morning TV and radio concerning her workshop "Communication for Married Couples," and has been interviewed on local university radio concerning her work with inner-city children.

Her research for the past six years has focused on using group-centered interventions with children who are having difficulty with reading. Dr. Clanton Harpine designed the motivational reading program, called "Camp Sharigan," which she has used extensively in her work and research over the past six years. She also developed the Reading Orienteering Club after-school program and the 4-step method for teaching first graders to read.

In recent years, Dr. Clanton Harpine has been teaching group therapy and counseling, life-span development, and human growth and development at the University of South Carolina–Aiken, and is continuing her research with group-centered interventions. She was selected for inclusion in *Who's Who of American Women,* 2006–2008, for her work with children in inner-city neighborhoods.

Introduction

Camp Sharigan meets two hours a day for five days. The camp features, a make-believe poison-ivy vine that captures tricky words. Children climb Mount Reading to find an adventure story, a fishing pole and magnet at Lake Read help children "hook onto" new books to read, stepping stones that lead to the rainbow bridge, a tent full of buzzing mosquitoes, a snake pit with warm fuzzy snakes that teach phonics, a puppet stage, pop-up houses, and camp cabins where children gather to write stories of their own. The Read and Hike Trail leads the children to books hidden under inflatable rocks, and a daily treasure hunt map sends everyone scurrying off in search of still another reading adventure. The Road to Nowhere but Reading is filled with funny stories, and a blazing paper campfire has books about food and healthy eating along with tasty snacks to sample. Also, there is the Camp Stop Sign where one has to stop to read a book.

Camp Sharigan is a week-long motivational reading clinic set in the atmosphere of a hands-on, wonder-filled summer camp and a perfect example of a group-centered intervention specifically designed for use in a school-based setting (Clanton Harpine, 2006). There are many different types of group interventions. Our focus is on school-based group interventions. Hoag and Burlingame (1997) state that more than 70 percent of children's counseling groups take place in schools. One of the primary concerns of group interventions in the schools is prevention (Kulic, Horne, & Dagley, 2004). Prevention theorists state that in order for group interventions to be effective in school-based settings they must be directly linked to academic performance (Greenberg, Weissberg, O'Brien, Zins, Fredricks, Resnick, & Elias, 2003). Therefore, as we build our theoretical base, we will build from the concept that to be effective our group intervention must be linked with academic performance in the classroom (Clanton Harpine, 2007a).

How do group-centered interventions help students? That is a complex question, but one that provides the central organizing principle throughout this book. It will be our contention that in order for a school-based group intervention to be effective with children, it must rebuild self-efficacy, fully utilize intrinsic motivation, and take advantage of the curative powers of group cohesion.

We will use examples throughout the book from the Camp Sharigan program to illustrate how a group-centered intervention can be used in a school-based setting. Using one example throughout the book provides continuity and will make it

E. Clanton Harpine, *Group Interventions in Schools.*
© Springer Science + Business Media, LLC 2008

easier to illustrate the implementation of theory and design with group interventions.

Using an example from a motivational reading program has another benefit from a counseling frame of reference because research has directly linked reading failure with classroom discipline problems, aggression, violence, delinquency, adolescent substance abuse, crime, dropping out of school, and the development of depression and anxiety (Catalano, Mazza, Harachi, Abbott, Haggerty, & Fleming, 2003; Greenberg, Domitrovich, & Bumbarger, 2001; Miller, & Shinn, 2005; Greene & Winters, 2006; Nastasi, Moore, & Varjas, 2004; Orfield & Lee, 2005; Prilleltensky, Nelson, & Pierson, 2001; Snowden, 2005; Twenge & Campbell, 2002). Learning to read is classified as the most important indicator of academic competence (Fleming, Harachi, Cortes, Abbott, & Catalano, 2004). When children's reading scores improve, children's mental and psychological well-being improves (Slavin & Madden, 2001). If we, as mental health professionals, can incorporate reading into our group-centered interventions, we can help children and teens turn away from dysfunctional behavior and prevent later developmental mental health problems.

We will say more about the role of reading in school-based mental health in Chapter 6, but for now, we will acknowledge its importance in the psychological well-being of all school-aged children and adolescents.

1
Erasing Failure with School-Based Prevention Programs

One cold and blustery morning, as I sat in the hallway pretesting prospective children for an after-school program, I noticed a cute little first-grade boy stomping down the hall to the principal's office. It was his third trip and the day had just begun. Throughout the week, the little boy maneuvered his way into trouble with several teachers. He got into trouble with the librarian as he walked in the door before school started; he got into trouble with the reading tutor on the playground at lunchtime; he again got into trouble with the reading tutor in the hallway after school while waiting for the bus. When I observed the child in the classroom, he jumped up out of his chair three times while the teacher was taking the lunch count, crawled across the floor chasing a pencil that he intentionally rolled off his desk, drew pictures on his desk with crayons, and even reached over to scribble on the worksheet of the boy who sat across from him. His list of offenses was long. This cute little first grader was to be one of 30 children assigned to my after-school program.

Six weeks later, his teacher greeted me in the hall, and said, "I can hardly believe my eyes; he sits at his desk, completes his work, and actually tries to avoid getting in trouble so that he doesn't get a detention after school and miss your program."

Academic failure is more than an educational problem. Failure in the classroom is also a psychological problem, because failure leads to low self-efficacy, behavior problems, and risky health decisions. When children lose the ability to cope with the pressures of the classroom and with peer pressure from friends, they no longer perceive that they have the ability to control their environment or to recover from setbacks, poor grades, or difficult situations in the classroom.

An attitude of failure is cumulative. Children develop an attitude of failure based on their past experiences (Bandura, Barbaranelli, Vittorio Caprara, & Pastorelli, 2001) and on their interactions with peers in the classroom (Nazroo, 2003). Once children experience failure (being placed in a low reading group, failing a spelling test, or any other event in which they fall below other children in the classroom), the belief that they will fail brings about low self-efficacy and more failure (Miech, Eaton, & Brennan, 2005). It becomes the responsibility of counselors and psychologists in school-based settings to provide psychological programs and interventions that address the stigmatizing effects of failure before they become developmental, behavioral, or motivational problems.

E. Clanton Harpine, *Group Interventions in Schools.*
© Springer Science+Business Media, LLC 2008

Group-centered interventions differ from other school-based programs in that group-centered interventions are linked to academic performance, which many consider essential in school-based mental health (Greenberg et al., 2003). The goal is to change how children learn and to replace negative thoughts and perceptions with positive action that they can take back to the classroom.

When we speak of erasing failure, it is not as a pencil erases marks on a paper, but as a process that the student works through in order to repair the damage inflicted through the stigmatizing label of failure. Insight or information alone is not enough. Children cannot overcome their perceptions that they are failures if they do not erase the pain and rebuild their self-efficacy; therefore, rebuilding self-efficacy becomes the first requirement of a successful group intervention.

Self-efficacy does not occur naturally in group process. Self-efficacy must be built into the group design. That is why merely placing children in a group after-school program that teaches classroom skills is not an effective group intervention, nor can it be an efficacy-rebuilding program.

Failure is a two-pronged problem. We must treat not only failure's emotional effects but also its cause. To erase or overcome the perception of failure, children must experience success in an efficacy setting in which the children's belief that they can accomplish the assigned task is rebuilt (Bandura, 1997). Success in individual one-on-one sessions often does not transfer back to the classroom, because interaction with peers is essential to rebuild efficacy (Pintrich & Schunk, 2002). In contrast, groups have demonstrated, through numerous studies, a high level of efficacy (Hoag & Burlingame, 1997). Group-centered interventions create a setting in which children can experience success and learn the necessary skills to transfer success back to the classroom.

Stigmatizing Labels

Children entering school are quickly labeled by teachers and peers (Oldfather, 2002). Such labels can have devastating effects on a child's development and adjustment throughout life (Deci, Vallerand, Pelletler, & Ryan, 1991). When children from at-risk populations start school, their development is often behind that of their peers, or they feel inferior to their peers. This perceived inferiority lessens the child's ability to learn (Buhs, Ladd, & Herald, 2006). If we can reverse this pattern of failure early and rebuild the child's desire to learn, we can make a difference in the child's ability to advance in school and succeed in life.

Children have basic psychological needs for belonging and competence (Baumeister & Leary, 1995); they require the fulfillment of these needs just as much as they need food and water if they are to grow and develop, and to maintain a state of mental well-being. Children believe that they can or cannot accomplish a particular task; the child's belief or expectation of success or failure will mobilize the child to attempt the task or refuse to try. This is why the group environment is so important; a positive group environment provides an incentive to try.

A competitive or judgmental classroom based on grades or testing instills fear of failure and therefore reduces the child's motivation to try. Persistence and effort are not synonymous terms in motivation, but both are essential. *Effort* means how hard the child is willing to try, and *persistence* means how long the child is willing to continue trying.

When a child's emotional problems are linked to classroom learning, the child must learn the necessary skills needed to return to the classroom and perform the desired task successfully. In addition, the child must learn how to erase the perception of failure (Zimmerman, 1995). Traditional counseling groups, although helpful, only tackle the emotional problems, not the learning deficits that caused the emotional problem to arise; children need help with both.

Research shows that children respond favorably to group counseling (Shechtman & Gluk, 2005). Counseling groups emphasize interaction, stress developing group cohesion, and focus on helping one another instead of competing. Group-centered interventions use the group counseling concept and add the therapeutic power of play and hands-on interactive skill development.

Group-Centered Interventions

Group-centered interventions do not fall into any of the established categories identified by the Association for Specialist in Group Work; they are not task groups, psychoeducational groups, counseling groups, or psychotherapy groups (Association for Specialists in Group Work, 2000). Nor can they be classified as a type of instruction (National Reading Panel, 2000). Group-centered interventions are designed to help children and adolescents in school-based settings alleviate an educational deficit, as psychoeducational groups do, but group-centered interventions do not rely on imparting information or group discussions.

Group-centered interventions structure the group's activities to maintain a positive working climate and to take advantage of interaction between participants. Group cohesion becomes one of the primary elements of change with a group-centered intervention. The focus is on the here and now, and participants learn and model appropriate classroom behavior as they interact together. The group becomes a miniature slice of society, stressing diversity, commonality, and acceptance, much as a counseling group does. Unlike counseling groups, group-centered interventions are action-oriented and use a hands-on approach. The group becomes a working laboratory where children and adolescents can learn new ways of solving problems. With children, an element of play is incorporated. This differs, however, from the traditional playroom stocked with symbolic toys as in play therapy. Instead, this is a structured motivational environment that uses manipulatives and hands-on group activities to change how children learn and function in the classroom.

Group-centered interventions combine therapeutic group process and intrinsic motivation in an atmosphere of play. Play is the medium through which children best interact. Intrinsic motivation leads to self-determination and engaged learning. Combining play, intrinsic motivation, and cohesion enables children to grow, learn, and change in a positive environment. For children labeled as at-risk, group-centered interventions can make the difference between success and failure.

Every year countless children succumb to the labels of *failure* or *at risk of failure* as they struggle in the classroom. My own research, stretching over the past six years from Dallas to the Bronx, shows that group-centered interventions can help to restore children to a state of psychological well-being and classroom success. I have worked with children who were expelled from the public school system in Tampa, children from the projects in Chicago, private and public school children in the Bronx, children from inner-city neighborhood schools in Ohio, Hispanic children in Texas, inner-city groups in Georgia, and rural at-risk children from poor neighborhoods in South Carolina.

Society faces a high nationwide dropout rate and an escalating rise in teenage violence and health risk behaviors. African-American children have a 50% dropout rate, the highest of any racial or ethnic group (Randolph, Fraser, & Orthner, 2004). Prevention programs are becoming more popular in school-based settings, and a growing body of evidence demonstrates the effectiveness of prevention programming (Adelman & Taylor, 2006; Brooks-Gunn, 2003; Nelson, Westhues, & MacLeod, 2003; Noam & Hermann, 2002).

Group interventions can play a part in helping children and teens learn to make wise decisions. The safety of a supportive, cohesive group is exactly what young people need to help them develop constructive problem-solving and decision-making skills.

As with the first grader mentioned in the introductory example, most behavior problems have an underlying cause. On the first day of the after-school program, the little boy in question arrived 30 minutes late because he had an after-school detention. Upon arriving, he plopped down in the corner of the room, pretending to ignore the other students. He was actually watching very intently. After about 40 minutes, he came over and asked me if he could join the other children. Throughout the remainder of the program, he was never late nor did he hesitate to participate.

Intrinsic motivation needs to be infused into every group-centered intervention. Intrinsic motivation is seen in the classroom when students complete a task because they want to rather than because they are required to or told to (Deci & Ryan, 1985). Group-centered interventions provide an environment conducive to change. In a school-based setting, group-centered interventions can be used before, during, or after school. A portable environment can be created in a classroom, library, or therapy room and can be moved from school to school. A portable play environment sets the stage for constructive therapeutic change. Such a group-centered intervention can be short-term, one week, or long-term, lasting the entire school year as needed by the participants.

Group-centered interventions combine group process, intrinsic motivation, and efficacy retraining in a positive, cohesion-centered program of change. The power of group process (Yalom & Leszcz, 2005) to move participants in a positive, life-fulfilling direction is what makes group-centered interventions successful.

In the case of the first grader who was perpetually in trouble, hands-on activities and the power of group process persuaded him to become involved. Once he became a full participant in the group, skill-building interventions alleviated his lack of ability to work effectively in the classroom, and the structured group process used in the after-school program helped him renew his confidence. He once again believed that he could perform the tasks that his teacher assigned; self-efficacy was restored. If his behavior had gone unchanged, his misdeeds would probably have escalated, continuing throughout his educational career.

A group-centered intervention was able to help this student change. A traditional counseling group would not have stressed skill-building or the hands-on interactive approach that proved to be so successful in this situation.

Group-centered interventions offer acceptance and emotional support while children work at changing and replacing dysfunctional patterns of learning with successful techniques and skills. Regardless of whether one is working with first-grade at-risk students or potential high school dropouts, group-centered interventions return the students to the classroom armed with new skills and the confidence to be successful. Creating a motivational environment becomes an essential step in this program of change.

One of the biggest problems facing public schools today is the pressure on administrators and teachers to get results on tests they are demanded to use. School-based mental health treatment often suffers under the demand for higher test scores. Teachers fear that students will miss out on classroom instruction if they participate in therapeutic programs. Parents fear that children will not perform satisfactorily on prescribed tests if they participate in "extra" counseling programs. The attraction of group-centered interventions is that they eliminate the need to worry about taking children away from content instruction. Group-centered interventions teach remedial skills in a motivational setting; therefore, students receive both therapeutic interventions and cognitive instruction. The goal, then, is to demonstrate how group-centered interventions can be built into prevention programs that overcome failure in the classroom and return children to successful, happy educational experiences.

Real-World Applications

Observational Extensions

Sit and watch children in a classroom as they go about their daily routine. Try to observe for at least an hour and select a class and teacher, if possible, where you are not known.

- What do you see happening?
- How do the children respond to the teachers' instructions?
- Are the children excited and happy?

- Do you see signs of failure in the classroom?
- What do the children need to do to be successful in this class?
- If behavior problems occur, what do you think caused the misbehavior?
- How would you change this classroom?
- What would you do differently, and why?

A Ready-to-Use Group-Centered Intervention: "Will You Go to the Grocery Store?"

This group-centered intervention works very well with children in the first and second grade. This is an excellent efficacy building, hands-on group intervention that motivates children who struggle in math to practice addition and subtraction.

Objective: To increase math skills through hands-on activities.

Time needed: 1 hour (can be expanded if desired).

Supplies needed: shopping lists (one for each child), grocery items (empty boxes), grocery shopping bags, price tags, play money (or make paper money), and pencils

1. Create a grocery store on a table or shelf. Make a large sign and print the name of the grocery store. Make a few sale signs of reduced prices or today's specials.
2. Collect empty food boxes and bags, such as cereal boxes. Make sure all boxes are clean. You can also save the paper wrapper from cans and tape them back together. Put together a collection of food items that children might enjoy shopping for, such as cookies, cereals, and crackers. Do not include any food. You want to encourage intrinsic motivation, not prizes or food rewards. Children will play the game just for the fun of shopping. Try to have only one of each food item. You do not want the children to compete or to grab food boxes ("I had it first").
3. Place price tags on each item.
4. Make a shopping list for each child. Write on the list the food item name exactly as it is on the box. Leave space on the shopping list for the children to add up how much money they have spent.
5. Give each child a designated amount of money (not real money), a shopping list, and a grocery bag.
6. The children must add the prices of the items on their list as they shop. Then they will subtract the cost of their grocery store items from the amount of money they have to spend.
7. At the checkout desk, you will help the children check their lists and their calculations.

2
Skill-Building Efficacy Retraining

As I approached the group, I noticed that participants were scattered throughout the room; no one sat with anyone else. I was working with a group that had labeled itself "The Outcasts." Others had repeatedly tried to work with this group. The group was defiant, self-serving, and accusatory. The members were convinced that someone else, not themselves, had caused their misery. I suggested that we form a drama club and write our own play. We practiced skits that demonstrated interpersonal conflicts to help create ideas, and we studied the format for writing a play. The group dove into writing a play with hostility and vengeance as their primary motives. We were able to meet for only an hour once a week, but the students soon started bringing in scenes that they had written at home. The writing process encouraged them to think reflectively, but the editing process, compiling all that they had written and selecting the material to use, was the most productive. Sometimes we acted out scenes and then discussed how the audience would receive them. This perspective taking, seeing their thoughts and actions through someone else's eyes, was very constructive. Rehearsals often spent more time talking about why someone would speak or think in a certain way than on performance techniques. On the afternoon of the performance, the students wanted to cancel it, claiming technical difficulties. They were afraid that their peers would not understand what they had written. The play was very much about their group and how they felt.

Their fears were unfounded. The play opened doors of understanding.

Many educational programs stress self-esteem, but children need more than high self-esteem to do well in the classroom. Children may believe that they are total failures without disliking themselves. Self-esteem is a judgment of self-worth, that is, whether you like or dislike yourself. Self-efficacy, however, is a judgment of personal capability, that is, whether or not one feels able to accomplish a particular task or perform a certain action.

There is no relationship between self-efficacy and self-esteem (Bandura, 1977). Efficacy, not self-esteem, accounts for academic success (Multon, Brown, & Lent, 1991). Efficacy fosters engagement (Schunk, 1991). Efficacy influences the effectiveness and consistency with which children apply what they know, and high self-efficacy affects the quality of children's thinking by increasing their persistence (Bandura, 1997). Efficacy is a key factor in preventing addictive and risky behaviors

E. Clanton Harpine, *Group Interventions in Schools.*
© Springer Science + Business Media, LLC 2008

(Petraitis, Flay, & Miller, 1995). Perceived self-efficacy is a controlling variable with behavioral intentions and behavior change (Schwarzer & Fuchs, 1995). Efficacy also affects moral and social development; therefore, efficacy should concern the classroom teacher, school counselor, psychologist, and, indeed, all practitioners who work with children.

Self-efficacy is the first essential component of any successful preventative group intervention program. A group intervention must strengthen self-efficacy to address the problem of academic failure successfully.

Rebuilding Self-Efficacy

Children's belief that they can work a math problem is a self-efficacy judgment. Self-efficacy is not a measurement of skills or abilities; instead, self-efficacy is your belief of what you can do with your skills and abilities. The self-assurance with which children approach a task influences whether they make good or poor use of their abilities. Success builds self-efficacy. Failure undermines children's self-efficacy, especially when failure occurs before they have time to establish a strong belief in their ability to succeed (Bandura, 1997). Children with a high degree of efficacy visualize themselves as being successful. Children who doubt their ability to accomplish a task (efficacy) visualize themselves as failures and dwell on what will go wrong instead of what they might accomplish. Children with low self-efficacy shy away from difficult tasks, put forth a weak commitment to accomplish goals, dwell on obstacles or problems, give up quickly, and perceive any setback or failure as a total failure (Bandura, 1995).

Play and Learning

Theorists have suggested since 1955 that children can be best educated through structured play activities, and that children can best learn to cope with developmental life tasks through an atmosphere of play (Axline, 1955; Frank, 1955; Lebo, 1955). Play therapy, for example, grew out of the need to help children express their feelings and problems. Children express their feelings and problems more comfortably through play because play is part of a child's natural developmental learning process. Group-centered interventions are not, however, just another play-based therapeutic technique for use with children and youth. Group-centered interventions have grown out of a need to help young people erase the stigmatizing effects of failure, rebuild self-efficacy, and rekindle developmental well-being so they can resume their place as positive, fully engaged participants in the classroom.

Both play-therapy and play-activity group counseling (Gazda, 1989) are frequently used in school-based settings. Although traditional group counseling and play-therapy groups have succeeded with various school-based problems, neither counseling nor play therapy has proven to be all that successful in dealing with academic classroom failure (Hellendoorn, Van der Kooij, & Sutton-Smith, 1994; Pumfrey & Elliot, 1970). Neither have they been completely successful for efficacy retraining (Fall, 1999; Ray, Bratton, Rhine, & Jones, 2001).

Group-centered interventions, however, are specifically designed to alleviate academic failure and rebuild self-efficacy. The advantage to using group interventions over traditional counseling is that group-centered interventions combine skill-building and intrinsic motivation to rebuild self-efficacy. Counseling groups in schools often stress developmental growth and focus on methods of prevention (Kulic, Dagley, & Horne, 2001), but do not teach academic skills. Group-centered interventions stress developmental growth, prevention, academic skills, and self-efficacy.

Developing a School-Based Efficacy-Retraining Program

Efficacy beliefs can be transformed from negative to positive through efficacy-retraining or structured programs where children experience success, but in order to do so, the programs must follow the basic principles of efficacy development. Albert Bandura (1995) lists four ways to develop a high degree of efficacy:

1. *Mastery experiences:* The efficacy retraining program must help the child develop the ability to overcome problems and obstacles. The program must offer more than just skills training, but, without skills, there can be no efficacy.
2. *Vicarious experiences:* Modeling and observing the success and perseverance of others who are viewed to be similar to oneself is extremely important in rebuilding self-efficacy. The task must be neither beyond the child's ability nor competitive; otherwise, self-efficacy will be lowered. In such a case, children will doubt their ability to repeat a difficult, even successful, action (Bandura, 1995). Therefore, ability and effort must be balanced and intertwined.
3. *Social persuasion:* The need to stress improving oneself instead of comparing oneself to others.
4. *Physiological and emotional states:* In an efficacy-retraining program, situational stressors, the child's mood, and previous experiences and perceptions must all play a role.

One way to apply Bandura's profile for a successful efficacy-retraining program is to look at an example of a group-centered intervention in relationship to efficacy retraining. A case study analysis helps illustrate how each of Bandura's steps can be applied to an actual program. Research about at-risk children has identified a strong relationship between efficacy and student achievement (Multon, Brown, & Lent, 1991). Academic failure, particularly low reading scores, has also been shown to predict violence and health risk behaviors in adolescence (Fleming et al., 2004; Hawkins et al., 1998). Since reading is one of the first, and often one of the most stigmatizing, aspects of classroom failure, our example will be a group-centered efficacy-retraining program for at-risk readers.

The Camp Sharigan Program: A Case Study

It is not enough for schools just to teach children how to read; schools must also develop programs that build self-efficacy. I spent four years developing the Camp Sharigan program during my work with inner-city children. My team and I traveled to Tampa, Chicago, Dallas, and the Bronx. Camp Sharigan follows Bandura's four principles. The first task was to create skill-building experiences that would help children master reading problems encountered in the classroom.

Mastery Experiences

An efficacy-retraining program must include skill-building activities that teach skills that the students have not learned in the classroom, but it must include more than that. As Bandura (1995) indicates, a successful self-efficacy program must also help the child learn ways to overcome problems and obstacles encountered in the classroom. Since research indicates that at-risk students are often not able to work well or achieve their full potential in a traditional classroom structure (Morris, Shaw, & Perney, 1990), it becomes essential to develop group-centered interventions to meet their needs.

Children learn through experience. The mere imparting of information is not enough; a child must experience the change. It is not enough to tell children that they are improving; children must see and experience that improvement. Encouraging a child who is not showing signs of improvement can actually harm the child's self-efficacy (Flammer, 1995).

Hands-on activities help children experience improvement. Camp Sharigan uses ten hands-on activities to increase intrinsic motivation: pop-up books, puppet plays, word games, storytelling, story writing, craft projects, funny stories, an unrestricted supply of books to choose from and read, story starters, and phonics games.

In developing Camp Sharigan, my goal was to create a fun, hands-on learning environment using group-centered structured play techniques, but I wanted these hands-on activities to go a step beyond just being fun, creative ways to learn; therefore, I designed hands-on structured play interventions that stressed more than just learning new classroom skills.

An example of a structured play intervention with therapeutic intent is capturing tricky words. Instead of working from the usual spelling list, where the teacher counts how many words the student spells incorrectly, a word that a child cannot pronounce, read, or spell becomes not a word missed but a new tricky word to capture and learn. The safe environment of play makes it okay not to be able to read or spell a word. Learning words becomes a game rather than a penalty. Without fear of embarrassment, children are more willing to be adventurous and try to learn.

Each time the children capture a tricky word, they follow a four-step method to learn the tricky word. With the help of the camp guide (a tutor stationed at each learning center) the children (1) sound out the word and use the word in a sentence, (2) tell the meaning of the word, (3) spell the word out loud, and (4) write the words they captured (missed) on a "poison-ivy" leaf and place their leaf on the poison-ivy vine around the room. The four-step learning process is essential to the tricky word concept. The group intervention would not work without the four-step method. When the two concepts are combined, this simple game helps children increase spelling, reading, and sight word proficiency (Clanton Harpine, 2005).

A paper poison ivy vine is used because poison ivy is often hard to identify in the woods; it is tricky, just as words are tricky. At Camp Sharigan, children are taught that they must be careful when identifying, spelling, or capturing tricky words so that they capture words correctly. The use of the words "poison-ivy vine" reminds children to be careful as they move from workstation to workstation. The concept of the poison-ivy vine is used as a fun way of tackling the cognitive process of learning new words.

Children enjoy capturing tricky words and adding them to the camp poison-ivy vine. At the end of the week, when the poison-ivy vine is measured to see how long it has grown, the children cheer when they see how many words they have captured. This structured play technique enables children who once feared spelling tests to shout in victory over the dreaded task. This is more than teaching a skill. This group-centered intervention reduces the sense of failure and anxiety often associated with spelling. It rebuilds self-efficacy by improving the children's belief that they can spell.

Vicarious Experience

Group-centered interventions must also allow children to observe their success and perseverance as they work with others in a group setting. When I began developing Camp Sharigan, the question was to determine how best to provide this modeling and observing experience with group process. Each task had to be both noncompetitive and appropriate for the child's skill level. To test various group approaches, my team and I went to struggling inner-city locations.

At the first site, the school used traditional reading groups of seven or eight students. The students were divided by age, but the reading circles did not work. The children could not read well enough to follow along in the book while someone else read.

We implemented story writing; having the children write their own stories was very effective. One student was threatening and belligerent when we arrived. When we left at the end of the week, he hugged us and promised that he would publish his own book some day.

Learning centers provide excellent vicarious experiences, but I also wanted to include the therapeutic power of group cohesion. I was worried that using learning centers would disrupt the therapeutic benefits of working together in a group. At our next location, twenty-four children came in the evening after school for a three-hour session. Four learning centers were scattered around one large room. The children rotated from table to table at designated intervals. At each learning center, the children worked on a specified reading assignment. They read and followed step-by-step directions for a different project at each station. The idea was to teach the children to read and follow simple craft directions to improve their comprehension.

We had the children make a pop-up book, and each evening ended with a puppet play, presented by the children. Motivation levels were high; two children even gave up their weekly bike-riding time to come to the reading clinic every night. The pop-up book project, completed in stages over an entire week, proved to be such an excellent motivator that children begged their parents each evening to let them return the next day so that they could complete another page in their book.

By the time we reached our third site, the program had expanded into a five-day, two-hour-a-day format, featuring ten learning centers. Helpers worked at each learning center. Treasure hunt maps directed everyone individually through the learning centers. Twenty-eight children, a mixture of first through third graders, came directly after school. The children usually worked in small groups that rotated between homework-based activities. The older children in particular enjoyed working at their own pace with the treasure hunt maps instead of being confined to just one group. The treasure hunt maps also distributed the group so that children did not move in clumps or clusters. There were never more than four or five children at a center at a time.

On the last day at our third site, the after-school group sponsoring the reading clinic held a parent program. The children worked all week to prepare a special puppet play for their parents. The play was about pollution. Children in the audience watched as child after child on stage tackled difficult pollution terms, learning to sound out confusing sounds instead of giving up. As one child in the group said, "I didn't think he could say that word. That's really good." He then picked up his puppet skit off the floor where he had thrown it, turned the page, and started practicing his own part in the play.

Camp Sharigan had become a vicarious experience where children could observe success and perseverance in others. This improves self-efficacy by letting the children see other children who are similar to themselves experience success.

At our next site, we instituted pre- and posttesting to ensure that children were actually improving in mastery of skills. The children showed improvement in spelling, reading, and sight words during the week-long reading clinic. They still sustained improvement one year later (Clanton Harpine & Reid, submitted 2008a).

Camp Sharigan combines silent and oral reading, puppets that teach phonics, and pop-up story books that encourage children to write their own stories. In addition to teaching new words, improving comprehension, and working with phonics, it employs group cohesion and interpersonal skill building to develop a complete efficacy-retaining program.

At Camp Sharigan, the students make their own pop-up books; this encourages them to write stories. Puppets, storytelling, and reading and following directions to complete the pop-up book provide an excellent modeling experience. Children who had no interest in reading were motivated to read the directions in order to work on the project.

Social Persuasion

The goal of Camp Sharigan is to maximize the therapeutic effects of group process and group cohesion. The program is challenging but not too hard; it is neither competitive nor comparative. Efficacy retraining and play are built into the program. It is a one week, ten-hour group intervention; therefore, the group process must be highly structured from the minute the children arrive until the minute they leave. Children must be able to see their self-improvement throughout the week in order for social persuasion to be successful.

Physiological and Emotional States

When children enter the classroom, they bring with them their personalities, self-concepts, efficacy beliefs, perceptions, and previous experiences, good and bad alike. The school, the teacher, the family, the community, and the classroom of peers all add to how children perceive their actions in the classroom.

Group-centered interventions provide a motivational environment in which children can learn basic skills and work at mastering a task at their own pace. The group serves as a medium to practice social skills, teamwork, and group participation.

Learning and change occur through group-centered interventions by structuring the child's behaviors. Action-oriented, hands-on learning centers and one-on-one remedial assistance, such as those used at Camp Sharigan, help children grow developmentally and learn more successfully. Challenging activities push the child to work slightly above their present level of development, thus learning new skills and solving old problems.

An atmosphere of play helps children learn by promoting growth and well-being, by helping children accomplish school objectives, and by enabling children to make adjustments in how they learn (Carmichael, 1991; Landreth, 2002). With group-centered interventions, children develop new pathways for learning material that they were unsuccessful in learning in the classroom.

A child's efficacy beliefs affect academic performance, cognitive skills, classroom coursework, and standardized testing (Schunk, 1989). Efficacy beliefs can differ from one subject to another, such as from math to reading. Cooperative classrooms can raise self-efficacy, while competitive classrooms lower self-efficacy. Children with high self-efficacy are more eager to participate in class, work harder on a task, and continue to work hard even when they encounter difficulties (Bandura, 1997; Zimmerman, 1995). When self-efficacious children encounter a word that they do not know, they will sound out the word, decipher the meaning faster, and persist at the task longer. They will also choose more challenging projects. Therefore, it is important to develop group interventions to help all children attain a high degree of self-efficacy.

Real-World Applications

Observational Extensions

Watch children as they read. Go to the library and watch children selecting books. How do they select a book? Are they careful not to disarrange the shelf or get the books out of order? Do they immediately open the cover of the book and begin to read? Or do they place their selected book on the table, talk to a neighbor, or look around the room?

Place a stack of books in a disarranged pile on the floor, dumped in a heap. Give children permission to look at the books. What happens? Do the children seem more enthusiastic sifting through a pile of disarranged books than searching for a book on a neatly organized library shelf? Why? What does this tell us about motivation? Do rules stifle motivation? How can we maintain order and discipline in the classroom or library, and yet encourage motivation at the same time?

A Ready-to-Use Group-Centered Intervention: "The Adventure"

Poor reading skills and poor comprehension often lead to classroom disruptive behavior. This group-centered intervention helps children increase their comprehension skills by applying and organizing details in a story.

This intervention was tested in a research study conducted in 2005 with at-risk readers. After the intervention, the at-risk readers outscored nonparticipants on a comprehension quiz (Clanton Harpine, 2005). The teachers also reported that participants returned to the classroom and worked more effectively after the intervention.

Objective: To increase comprehension skills through hands-on activities.
Time Needed: 1 hour

1. Read the story (see below) to the children.
2. Have the children complete the story by writing their own ending.
3. Have the children draw a map, which illustrates the path that Mr. Bear and his friends took on their adventure.
4. Have the children discuss their story endings and maps.

The Story: "The Adventure"

Mr. Bear was bored. He was tired of getting up every morning and not having anything to do. "I need an adventure," said Mr. Bear. "I want to go and do something exciting," he said to himself. "But what can I do?"

Mr. Bear thought and thought. "Maybe I can build a new house," he said. "No, it takes too long to build a house and besides building a house is very hard work. I want to go on an exciting adventure. Maybe I can go shopping and buy something new. No, I don't want to go shopping. I'm tired of shopping," said Mr. Bear to himself. "I want to go and do something I have never done before. I want … I want … I want to cross the lake."

Mr. Bear lived on the north side of a large lake. He could not see across the lake because the lake was too wide. Mr. Bear could not see the ends of the lake because the lake was too long. The lake stretched as far as anyone could see.

Mr. Bear had always been curious about what lay beyond the lake, but he had never been to the other side. "That's it," he said. "I'll be an explorer and travel south across the lake and see what is on the other side. I'll have a grand adventure," said Mr. Bear.

Mr. Bear went into his cave house and began to pack for his trip across the lake. He packed a toothbrush, comb, change of clothes, and a compass. "I don't want to get lost," said Mr. Bear to himself.

"I'll need a friend. I need someone to share my adventure with," said Mr. Bear.

Mr. Bear went down to the edge of the lake where the beavers had made a small pond on the side near the trees. Mr. Bear waded out to the beaver dam and knocked politely.

Benjamin Beaver poked his head up out of the lookout hole. "Good morning, Mr. Bear," said Benjamin Beaver pleased to see his friend on such a bright and sunny morning. "What brings you over to my humble abode?" asked Benjamin Beaver.

"I'm going on a grand and glorious adventure," said Mr. Bear. "I'm going to cross the lake. Would you like to come along?"

"Cross the lake! No, never," said Benjamin Beaver. "Why would I be foolish enough to try and cross the lake? That's nonsense. If we were meant to cross the lake we would have been born on the other side. We are meant to live on this side of the lake. I have absolutely no plan to ever cross the lake. There's no telling what's out there. There could be monsters living in that lake. No, no, I most definitely don't want to cross the lake, and you shouldn't cross it either."

"I'm bored," said Mr. Bear. "I want to see what is on the other side. I need an adventure."

"Better to be bored than lost" said Benjamin Beaver.

"I won't get lost," said Mr. Bear. "I'm bringing my compass."

"I won't go with you," said Benjamin Beaver shaking his head. "I have trees to gnaw down. I need to expand the lodge. I don't have time for such foolishness as crossing the lake. If you intend to waste your time, you must go alone."

Mr. Bear waded back to shore as Benjamin Beaver dove back down underneath the water. Mr. Bear crawled out of the pond dripping wet and walked on his hind legs over to the old hollow oak tree. Mr. Bear knocked politely again.

Blue Jay stuck his head out and said, "What do you want?"

"I'm sorry; I didn't mean to disturb you," said Mr. Bear. "I'm going on a great and wonderful adventure, and I just wanted to know if you would like to go along?"

"Where are you going?"

"I'm going to cross the lake," said Mr. Bear.

"Cross the lake! Why on earth would you want to cross the lake? Do you have any idea what is out there?"

"No, that's why I want to go. I want to know what lies on the other side of the lake. Will you go with me?"

"I have been to the other side," said Blue Jay.

"You have? What's it like? Did you like it? When did you go?"

"It wasn't worth the trip, and I don't want to go again," said Blue Jay.

"Oh please," said Mr. Bear. "It would be wonderful to have a friend and a guide on the trip. And since you have been before, you'd know the best route to take. We'd have a wonderful time."

"Well, it might be fun, but it's dangerous. Are you sure you want to cross the lake?"

"Yes, I'm certain," said Mr. Bear.

"Very well then," said Blue Jay. "I'll go with you and be your guide."

"Fantastic!"

"What's fantastic?" said little Sister Bear, who came bouncing over the hill in pursuit of a butterfly that easily escaped her grasp.

"Blue Jay and I are going on an adventure together. We're going to cross the lake," said Mr. Bear.

"Oh goody," said little Sister Bear. "I want to go. too."

"No, it'll be much too dangerous for you. We must go alone," said Mr. Bear.

Little Sister Bear began to cry.

"Very well, don't cry. You can go," said Mr. Bear.

"Goody, goody, goody," said Sister Bear. "I must go and pack."

"Pack? Pack what? Who's packing?" said Tuffy Turtle, poking his head out of his shell to see what the excitement was about.

"I am," said Sister Bear. "We're going on an adventure. You should come too."

"Never!" said Blue Jay. "Do you have any idea how long it takes to cross the lake and how slow Tuffy is? We'll never get across the lake if we have to wait on him."

"Well, that's just too bad," said Sister Bear. "You're never supposed to leave anyone out. If one gets to go, then we should all get a chance to go. Otherwise, we all have to stay home. That's the rule."

Everyone was silent for a minute. Then Mr. Bear said, "It'll be great to have you along, Tuffy. Hurry, go pack!"

As the four set out on their adventure, Blue Jay rode on top of Mr. Bear's head so that he could be the lookout. Tuffy clamped onto Sister Bear's fur so that she could pull him along as she swam. Mr. Bear and Sister Bear sank down into the lake and began to swim.

Little Sister Bear was a strong swimmer for her age, but she soon began to get tired. Everywhere you looked there was water, with no place to rest.

Blue Jay seemed to sense Mr. Bear's concern as Sister Bear began to drop further and further behind. "Will we reach the other side soon?" asked Mr. Bear.

"No, not for awhile; it'll be a long swim. We've barely begun," said Blue Jay. "But there is a small island just ahead. We can't stop for long, but maybe just a minute to rest. It's not safe; so we need to be extra quiet and only rest for a few minutes."

Discussion with the Children

"You're the authors. Will the four stop to rest at the island? What will happen while they are on the island? Who will they meet? What happens next?"

3
Motivation: Intrinsic vs. Extrinsic

From the minute he walked through the door, he was primed and looking for a fight. His back was stiff; tension rippling through his body, and he walked with a swagger. He pushed and shoved, demanding to sit at the front, and then began to curse when he did not get what he wanted. Only a third grader, he was rapidly developing a reputation.

I separated him from the rest of the group and instructed him to sit alone for five minutes. I told him that I'd be back to talk with him. He shouted from across the room, "I'm not coming tomorrow; you'll never see me again."

By the end of the session, he was sitting beside me, working on a challenge step. When I told him that I hoped to see him again tomorrow, he said, "Don't worry. I'm coming. Do you think I could work on another challenge step tomorrow?"

Motivation can be defined as the internal driving force that explains why we do what we do. Motivation may be constructive or destructive. This internal force arises from the child's perceptions of self and others and the environment in which the child lives and works. There is a need, an understanding of that need, and an emotional drive that energizes the child from within, and that either encourages or discourages the child from engaging in a particular action or behavior (Reeve, 1993).

The young third-grader presented his tough-guy defense to protect himself from a new situation that he found threatening. Children who do not have strong relationships with their peers struggle academically (Wentzel, 2003), compounding problems in the classroom. Low self-efficacy and fear of failure are often hidden behind a tough-guy veneer. It is more acceptable with peers to get in trouble for your behavior than it is to be shown to fail academically. If we do not reverse such behavior in the early stages of the educational process, we must then contend with teenagers who take pride in their failure and maintain group status through being a failure.

The Need for Intrinsic Motivation

Very few children are intrinsically motivated to form straight lines when walking down the hallway at school, but, as the third grader in the opening example proved, behaviors can be changed. The environment in which the child is learning often determines whether that behavior is desirable or undesirable. The type of motivation used to encourage children to learn a specific behavior will be successful only if it helps fulfill normal intrinsic desires and curiosities. Children may be motivated to misbehave to get attention from their peers when they do not know the answer to a question or fear that they will fail at a task. Or children may be motivated to change their behavior, adopt the rule structure of the classroom, and learn a new constructive task.

Children's self-worth becomes linked to efficacy through their ability to accomplish a prescribed task and through interactions with others in their environment. Children become, to some extent, products of their environment, but they also produce and interpret their environmental experiences (Schunk & Pajares, 2005).

Children are born with an internal desire to learn (Sternberg, 2000). Normal growth and development is best supported by learning that allows children to explore and discover through their actions (Rogers, 1969). Intrinsic motivation occurs when a person responds to an internal need, to curiosity, or to an internal desire (Deci & Ryan, 1985). It is the environment in which children live and learn that provides or fails to stimulate this intrinsic need.

Environment Is an Essential Component of Motivation

Even young children who experience limited stimulation from their environment typically learn to walk and talk. Internal needs generate the motivation that propels a child into action, but sometimes children are passive or expect society to supply the motivation. Research indicates that such placidity may be a learned state (Ryan & Deci, 2000).

Self-efficacy plays a major role in motivation. Children perceive environmental experiences as encouraging or discouraging based on their efficacy, that is, on their belief that they can or cannot accomplish the task (Bandura & Cervone, 2000). Perceived control over one's environment is a key motivator in life (Bandura, 1986). Perceived control leads to a sense of self-determination, which involves the internalization and acceptance of the environment's external rule structure (Rigby, Deci, Patrick, & Ryan, 1992).

The third grader in our opening example came from an abusive home and was accustomed to attacking everyone in every situation before they had an opportunity to attack him. When confronted with a new, threatening experience for which he was uncertain of his abilities, his initial response was to attack. A group-centered intervention, through the use of intrinsically motivating activities, gave the boy an opportunity to explore and make choices, all the while requiring him to conform to the group structure and rules. He maintained a sense of perceived control while accepting the group intervention's external rule structure.

The environment created by a group-centered intervention becomes an essential part of the motivating process. An intrinsically motivating environment can actually change how children perceive themselves as learners and as participants in a group. Intrinsic motivation can help children rebuild their self-efficacy, change their approach to learning, and, consequently, change their behavior.

Therefore, our second essential component of a successful preventative group intervention program is intrinsic motivation. If we are to build and develop successful group interventions, such interventions must include intrinsic motivation.

Motivation in the Classroom

Imagine how hard it would be to sit in a classroom day after day trying to muster the motivation to read or work a math problem if you were convinced beforehand that you could not. In school, most teachers use candy, stickers, pizza parties, or other extrinsic rewards to motivate children. But such rewards discourage children. Research has shown that teaching children to perform a task for an award or prize encourages children to complete the task only when they receive a reward, or to select easier tasks so they can receive the reward faster (Fawson & Moore, 1999).

Extrinsic motivation comes from the environment, not the individual. Extrinsic motivation is usually in response to a prize or reward, or it may be to avoid an undesirable consequence. When extrinsic rewards and prizes are used in the classroom, research shows that children are often not motivated to complete a task or to try again until they are offered another prize (Deci et al., 1991). The quality of learning suffers, motivation suffers, and it is not long before failure sets in (Benware & Deci, 1984). The use of prizes and awards as motivators reduces a child's natural intrinsic desire to learn (Swann & Pittman, 1977).

Children learn to work only for expected awards and to focus on producing a correct answer to please the teacher or to receive a reward rather than to discover the joy of learning new information (Henderlong & Lepper, 2002). When the prize or award is removed, children drop back to their premotivational level of performance, or sometimes even below (Lepper & Greene, 1975). This results in children applying less effort and persistence than before the prizes or awards were offered. Teaching children to perform for food or prizes tends to encourage children to work just enough to get the prize and then quit (Thorkildsen, 2002).

For children to be successful in school, they must have the internal desire to learn, and to choose on their own to learn rather than being forced (Baker, Dreher, & Guthrie, 2000; Deci, Ryan, & Williams, 1995; Greenberg et al., 2001).

Motivation is often misunderstood in educational circles; therefore, it becomes the role of psychologists to demonstrate how motivation works in school-based settings. It is important to encourage children without extrinsic rewards or prizes. Intrinsic motivators can be built into the classroom structure and into a group intervention. Successful group interventions should stimulate a child's desire to learn and boost a child's self-efficacy.

Achievement and self-regulation are linked to self-efficacy (Schunk, 1991; Zimmerman & Martinez-Pons, 1988). If we want to teach children to learn for the love of learning, then we must give more attention to how we motivate children in the classroom.

Intrinsic Motivation Encourages Children to Learn

Children are born with a natural desire to explore, investigate, discover, and learn. Yet, all too often, this natural developmental desire declines during the educational process (Dweck, 2000). When the educational environment builds on children's natural curiosity, offers challenges, and stimulates the interest that energizes learning, then children will be engaged in learning. It is not part of the normal and natural development of children to be motivated to sit still, be quiet for long periods of time, or do repetitive routine class and homework assignments. Children learn through their actions. This is not always conducive to a quiet, orderly classroom. The challenge, then, is how to combine the needs of the educational system with the needs of the developing child.

Children's experiences in the classroom are of vital importance to the psychologist, because the way in which children learn in the classroom affects not only their acquisition of educational knowledge but also their emotional adjustment and psychological well-being today and throughout their life span (Elliot & Dweck, 2005). Schools shape self-esteem, coping strategies, social development, personal values, and self-efficacy (Schunk, 1995).

The problem is how can we use the extrinsic structure of the classroom to encourage self-regulated learning and intrinsically motivated inquiry. One suggestion is to free children from rewards and punishments and to reestablish discovery rather than "learning about" a subject (Deci & Ryan, 1985). The classroom climate must be informational rather than controlling if intrinsic motivation is to thrive (Deci, Nezlek, & Sheinman, 1981). By informational, Deci et al. mean that the classroom allows the child to learn through exploration and discovery rather than simply rote memorization.

Self-Determination

Active learning in a positive classroom environment does not mean that children should be free to do whatever they wish. A classroom structure can be created that supports both intrinsic motivation and self-determination. Self-determination requires learning to work harmoniously within the classroom structure.

Intrinsic motivation need not be destroyed in the classroom as long as children are allowed an element of choice (Koestner, Ryan, Bernieri, & Holt, 1984). On the one hand, intrinsic motivation improves the quality of learning and achievement in content areas (Deci & Ryan, 1985), and correlates positively with achievement test scores (Connell & Ryan, 1985). On the other hand, the mention of monetary awards or upcoming exams reduces comprehension of material (Deci & Ryan, 1985). Therefore, when classroom conditions are conducive to intrinsic motivation, learning improves (Deci & Ryan, 1985). The task that remains, then, is for the classroom teacher to create an intrinsically motivating classroom environment.

School counselors and psychologists can help with this process by teaching the importance of intrinsic motivation and by creating group interventions with an intrinsic focus. After-school programs are excellent alternatives that allow for the creation of group-centered interventions that stress intrinsic motivation.

Developing an Intrinsically-Based Group-Centered Intervention: A Case Study

Let us return to our example of the Camp Sharigan motivational reading program. How is intrinsic motivation used at the camp?

At Camp Sharigan, children uncurl paper grapevines and try to read as far as they can until they capture (miss) five words. The five captured words are new words for them to learn. There is no competition or prize. Each word captured is added to the poison-ivy vine strung around the room, and it is simply a means of self-satisfaction and intrinsic desire to improve. The children are thrilled at the end of the week when they count how many words they have captured.

The children also work and solve word problems presented by the puppets each day, and the puppet plays work perfectly as long-term intrinsic motivators. Even if children struggle to read, they are still eager to get involved with the puppet play.

A third intrinsic motivator is to have the children write stories. Sometimes they are asked to finish a story; other times they write their own versions of a story. The emphasis on reading and following directions works well to increase comprehension. Action stories at the opening of each session emphasize listening and interpersonal skills.

Making a pop-up book is a week-long motivator that encourages children to work all week writing and creating their own special pop-up story. The children practice writing skills, editing their stories, and reading and following directions to make their book.

Camp Sharigan uses hands-on intrinsically motivating activities to teach academic skills while rebuilding self-efficacy and motivating children to return to the classroom ready to learn. Intrinsic motivation cannot thrive in a stifling environment. Hands-on projects allow children to learn through their actions and to use their naturally occurring intrinsic curiosities.

Six Principles for Designing Intrinsically Motivating Group Interventions

Intrinsic motivation does not happen automatically. To take full advantage of the therapeutic power of intrinsic motivation, a group intervention must adhere to six basic motivational principles: positive self-efficacy, efficacy expectations, outcome expectations, choice, competence-affirming feedback, and self-determination.

1. *Positive self-efficacy:* Positive success must replace negative feelings or expectancies of failure. The first step is positive thinking. Children have to see improvement, such as in word skills during the week, before they will begin to perceive themselves to be strong readers. The grapevine at Camp Sharigan allows children to see themselves progress each day as they read further and further up the grapevine. It's not competitive; there's not a grade. There are several grapevines the child can choose from. Therefore, the chosen grapevine becomes intrinsically motivating, helping to create a positive atmosphere of competence in which self-efficacy can be rebuilt. Everyone's reading, but no one's competing with anyone else.

2. *Efficacy expectations:* Simply learning new words is not enough to change a child's efficacy expectations about reading. Children must exercise control over their own reading development. Step-by-step progressive activities and the fun nature of Camp Sharigan motivate the children to tackle harder reading tasks. The children use stepping stones at the Rainbow Bridge in Camp Sharigan. Children decide to read a step 1, step 2, step 3, or step 4 level book. Children are encouraged to move up a step each time they can successfully read a book. Children get excited to discover a new story hidden beneath the next stepping stone, and they enjoy hopping from stepping stone to stepping stone as they advance in reading. But it's not competitive; the stepping stone activity is not a group venture. Each child works individually with a tutor. There is no comparison between children and no identification of the child's reading level. As children improve over the week, they are more willing to try new, harder reading tasks. Skill-level appropriate activities in phonics, word recognition, and comprehension increase the child's confidence and ability as a reader.

3. *Outcome expectations:* To produce personal motivation, with high effort and strong persistence, children need to expect success. Short-term, easy projects help accomplish this. The tasks do not carry any reward or punishment. The children are able to reach a goal by reading and following directions; therefore, their outcome expectations rise. Each day, Camp Sharigan provides both easy and challenging activities, and many of the activities, such as the Camp Cabin allows for individual creativity. The children complete the Camp Cabin project in three easy steps by cutting a roof pattern and gluing two pieces of paper together to make a house. Children draw windows, doors, trees, or other desired decorations, or they may cut and glue elaborate decorations from bits and pieces of construction paper for their camp cabin.

4. *Choice:* Self-efficacy is about choice: which activities do the children feel comfortable and confident enough to try. In addition, how much effort or persistence are the children willing to exert, and how do the children cope with stress? Making pop-up books provides first through third graders with an excellent challenge. The book is designed with stages of development in mind. The children must exert control to cut, fold, and manipulate the paper into shapes that pop up to make the desired project. The children may also decide how many pages they wish to have in their pop-up books. One book might have two pages, while another might have six. Again, there is no competition. The project is designed

so that each page, in and of itself, creates a complete project. Increased effort provides increased self-satisfaction. Every child makes a unique book.

5. *Competence-affirming feedback:* All children want to be successful, to feel as if they are improving, and to experience progress. To feel competent is a basic psychological need. Since success is emotionally rewarding, it is itself a strong motivator. Children derive great pleasure from their accomplishments. There can only be progress for the child, never failure, in a successful efficacy-retraining program. Puppet plays fulfill this task at Camp Sharigan. The children experience satisfaction from being puppeteers in the puppet plays. Very shy children listen for their puppet to speak, and then present their puppet at the proper time in the story. Older, more confident children enjoy reading the puppet skits and using character voices. A puppet play allows everyone to succeed. It encourages children to challenge themselves to do harder tasks than they might otherwise perceive themselves capable of completing.

6. *Self-determination:* For children to become self-directed readers, they must make the choice to read rather than watch television, and to decide to add reading to their daily schedules. For this to happen, children must perceive reading to be a fun, stimulating activity. By structuring the nature of the group experience and the feedback children receive from peers and workers at the camp, Camp Sharigan shapes the rebuilding of self-efficacy. To build a strong, positive self-efficacy, children must develop self-regulatory skills. They must develop skills that influence motivation and behavior, set attainable goals, and direct their behavior toward learning new skills. Intrinsic motivators raise children's self-expectations and empower children to become more self-directed.

Children who bear the label "at risk" need to rebuild not only their desire to learn but also their personal feelings of competence. Therefore, skills training combined with intrinsic motivation must be an integral part of every group-centered intervention.

Real-World Applications

Observational Extensions

Watch children working together on a project. Then, observe children sitting in silent rows in a classroom. Which group seems more intrinsically motivated?

A Ready-to-Use Group-Centered Intervention: "The Puppets Say"

Many children misbehave in the classroom or sit stubbornly for hours, even through recess, refusing to write when given a writing assignment, simply because they fear failure. I use this group-centered intervention with children who struggle with writing assignments in the classroom.

Objective: To increase writing skills through hands-on activities.

Time needed: 1 hour (Can be expanded if desired).

Supplies needed: empty plastic water bottle for each student (individual size), flesh-colored construction paper for faces (one sheet per student), glue, construction paper for hair, scissors, and markers or crayons.

1. Give each student an empty water bottle and a piece of flesh-colored construction paper.
2. Tell students that they are going to make a puppet.
3. Glue flesh-colored construction paper around the water bottle. Glue paper to the bottle. The cap of the water bottle will become the handle for the puppet. Make sure paper does not cover up the handle.
4. Have students decorate their puppet's face. Use markers to draw a face.
5. Hair can also be made from construction paper. Write names on bottle caps with a permanent marker. Set puppets aside to dry.
6. Have students work in groups of three to five members to write a puppet play.
7. Have each group member give his or her puppet a name and talk about the puppet's favorite activity. Ask the group to write a puppet play using the puppets. (Often, young children will write a story rather than a play skit; that's okay. The idea is to encourage children to write. If you have a story rather than a puppet skit, have a narrator read the story as the other children perform with their puppets.)
8. Work with each group to edit the puppet skits before the children perform them. Remove any violence and rude words. This is an excellent chance to work on sentence construction and grammar. Make sure that the puppet performances are a positive experience for everyone.
9. Allow children to read and perform their puppet play. If you do not have a puppet stage in your room, you may have two children hold up a blanket. Those performing can hide behind the blanket, holding up their puppets.

4
Group Process and Change

The director introduced me to the children, and told me that the group had been disbanded because of behavior problems. "They are just impossible to work with," she said. At my first meeting with the group, when I introduced the concept of clowning, explaining that we would go to hospitals and nursing homes to visit shut-ins, only three members attended. I encouraged them to wear an old shirt to the next meeting because we would be experimenting with clown makeup. At the second meeting, thirteen children came. Each member had to decide on a clown name and a design for his or her clown face. Group members were invited to create a clown costume out of old clothes and wear their costume to the next meeting. By the third meeting, there were twenty-six in attendance, all arriving in an assortment of costumes. We practiced clown routines and made name tags, using their clown names. We then applied our clown makeup and left for the nursing home. The group met for over a year, spreading joy to hospitals, nursing homes, and anyone in need. The group not only helped others but also helped themselves, because through clowning they learned to care about and to help the other members of the group. This dysfunctional, bad behavior group turned into one of the most positive and supportive of youth peer groups.

Groups form a microcosm of life, a slice of the real world where children and teens can experiment interpersonally and grow, but group experiences can be either positive or negative. Just because people join a group, even a school-based group does not mean that they will have a positive experience. For example, researchers have documented a direct increase in alcohol consumption for participants in teenager's athletic teams (Barber, Eccles, & Stone, 2001; Eccles & Barber, 1999), and having a religious affiliation does not always deter sexual behavior (Donnelly, Duncan, Goldfarb, & Eadie, 1999). All the same, as in our example above, a dysfunctional group can become a positive peer group influence. To create positive group experiences, we must understand how group process works.

   Successful group interventions must include cohesive group process, because cohesiveness is essential for the development of an atmosphere in which the curative factors of change can work and be successful (Marmarosh, Holtz, & Schottenbauer, 2005). So the third essential ingredient of a successful preventative group intervention program is to use group process to bring about individual change.

E. Clanton Harpine, *Group Interventions in Schools.*
© Springer Science+Business Media, LLC 2008

The Need to Belong to a Group

A group is more than just a collection of people; it is an interpersonal social structure that develops and maintains a culture all its own. All group members have the same basic psychological needs: the need to belong, to feel secure and accepted by others, to have a sense of control or personal accomplishment, and the safety to interact with others to establish a sense of self-identity (Hogg, Abrams, Otten, & Hinkle, 2004). The solidarity and cohesiveness of a group result from the group's ability to satisfy its members' psychological needs. Competition may help a group pull together to complete a short-term task, but, over a long period, competition can and will destroy a group's solidarity and cohesion (Deci & Ryan, 1985).

Group members need to feel special. Cohesion is a must. Optimal interaction that encourages participation and decision making by group members will help to build a cohesive group. The more cohesive the group is, the more social pressure it exerts on its members, and the more likely it is to bring about change and conformity to social standards in a school or community (Abrams, Rutland, & Cameron, 2003).

Cohesion is more than just people being attracted to or liking other group members. Cohesion is actually a sense of belonging, a relationship among group members that includes trust and a desire to be kind to those within the group, as well as understanding and positive acceptance of other group members (Yalom & Leszcz, 2005). Each group member brings to the group a sense of self-identity. This self-identity arises from past experiences and future goals. Our feelings and values are two of the most important determinants of how we act and behave (Levy, 1972). This positive, cohesive sense of belonging is necessary for change to occur. Self-disclosure signifies that a group is cohesive. Acceptance of self and acceptance of other group members, even those who may be quite different, is essential in a cohesive group. Self-acceptance is the beginning of change (Rogers, 1976). Cohesion must be built from within group process through positive interactions among group members. Competition and arguments do not lead to cohesion. The members of a cohesive group must be accepting of one another and must work toward a common goal that benefits all group members. A destructive group process is not conducive to positive change, while cohesion helps to bring about positive change in group process.

Increasing the amount of time that the group members work together on a long-term project helps to maximize the impact group process can have for bringing about change and conformity. A healthy, cohesive group encourages members to think and act creatively, to be innovative, and to explore different ways of solving a problem. Motivation is strongest when group accomplishments can be attributed to the efforts of the group as a whole rather than the efforts of one or two individuals. To succeed, group members must establish and maintain satisfactory interpersonal relationships with the other members of the group. There is a need to belong, to be wanted by the other group members, and, in turn, to care about and show interest in the other members of the group.

Change Through Group Process

Groups can be used to bring about a change in behavior, achievement, and psychological well-being with children and teens (Finn, Gerber, & Boyd-Zaharias, 2005), but change does not happen automatically. You cannot simply create a group and think that it will bring about a positive change. If the group is to serve as a venue for positive change, the necessary elements must be built into the group from its very beginning.

Change is the central variable around which the success or failure of a preventative group intervention must be measured (Kulic et al., 2004)—not only change within the group but also change that transfers back to the classroom (Obiakor, 2001). For a school-based group intervention to succeed, the intervention must facilitate change, which must then transfer back to the classroom and continue over time. Temporary change, such as change that only occurs during the intervention, does not lead to well-being throughout life (Duckworth, Peterson, Matthews, & Kelly, 2007). What we seek is change that will help children today and tomorrow.

How Does Group Process Bring About Change?

Irvin Yalom identifies eleven therapeutic factors that lead to change in therapy groups (Yalom & Leszcz, 2005). Just as a therapy group should facilitate change, a school-based group intervention must also facilitate change through group process.

Group interventions use group process in much the same way as therapeutic groups, except that group-centered interventions emphasize hands-on skill-building to rebuild self-efficacy and intrinsic motivation to create change that transfers back to the classroom. We will look at how group-centered interventions use group process through comparison to Yalom's eleven therapeutic factors of change: hope, universality, imparting information, altruism, the family group, socializing techniques, imitative behavior, interpersonal learning, group cohesiveness, catharsis, and existential factors (Yalom & Leszcz, 2005).

Hope

Hope is essential with group interventions. Positive thinking and positive expectations are necessary in order for children and teens to be willing to become involved in a group. The element of play excites children and motivates them to get involved in the group. An imaginative atmosphere is part of healing (Malchiodi, 2005). Active involvement and creating hands-on projects energize, redirect, and refocus misbehavior for children who struggle in the classroom. The excitement of completing a difficult task, one that once seemed impossible, becomes a beacon of hope.

For teens, community service can be coupled with group process to facilitate change. Working to help others emphasizes leadership, moral development, and real-world application. Teen service teams work with at-risk children, go to nursing homes, or visit the pediatric ward at the hospital. Organizing and planning service projects encourages growth. Creating an atmosphere of hope instills a desire for change.

Universality

Children who are considered to be at risk of failing often feel that they are the only ones who struggle in the classroom. Teens who feel rejected, who feel left out by the in-crowd, perceive that they will never find acceptance, never find anyone who will care about them, never find a group in which they can belong. All of us have this fear of inadequacy, and it is only through finding acceptance that we are able to control the fear. If we do not control the fear of inadequacy, then it can begin to dominate, to control our lives, and to lead to mental health problems. Mental illness grows out of inadequate interpersonal interactions and relationships (Yalom & Leszcz, 2005). If children and teens get help, they learn that everyone struggles; they no longer feel isolated or overwhelmed by the difficulties of functioning in the real world. Self-expression can be a corrective experience (Landreth, 1991). Working together in a positive group environment can help children and teens find acceptance. Acceptance can lead children and teenagers to change unwanted behaviors. For a group intervention to succeed and to foster change, it must offer acceptance.

Information

Groups are often the setting for learning new information. In traditional therapy groups, this is often through didactic instruction or direct advice. With school-based group-centered interventions, information is imparted through structured hands-on activities. At Camp Sharigan, children learn phonics, spelling, and basic reading skills through hands-on activities at each learning center. With the middle-school group intervention described at the beginning of this chapter, the teens learned to understand each other, to think of the needs of others, and to interact acceptably with peers through the hands-on process of developing a clown troupe. Modeling appropriate behavior is part of the information sharing process. Creative expression helps children and teens learn to handle their feelings and problems effectively (Gladding & Newsome, 2003).

Altruism

Group process allows children and teens to help others. There is something curative about serving and fulfilling the needs of others. The shift between receiving help and providing help for others is also therapeutic (Holmes & Kivlighan, 2000). As Victor Frankl (1969) stated most eloquently, true meaning in life cannot be obtained through deliberate pursuit; we must turn away from concern and worry about ourselves, and instead, become absorbed in the needs of someone else. The group focus of a group-centered intervention strives to accomplish this need to help others, through service projects and through the process of working together in small groups to accomplish a task. Working in small groups allows children and teens to help their classmates instead of competing with other group members. Learning to work together as a team, instead of competing with one another, is conducive to change.

The Family Group or Classroom: A Reflection of Interpersonal Problems

Group interventions reflect classroom and peer group behaviors. Children who have trouble interacting and following rules in the classroom will bring those same behavior patterns to the group-centered intervention.

Remember the precocious little first grader from Chapter 1 who was always in trouble? On his first day, he refused to participate. He sat in the corner. It was the emphasis on play that encouraged him to get involved instead of misbehaving as usual. Once he got involved with the group, the group's cohesion encouraged him to change his behavior and work with his teacher and classmates in the group and in the classroom.

Transforming a bad-behavior group into a clown troupe to visit nursing homes and hospitals helps teenagers examine their self-image. Reflection, together with the creation of a new clown personality, helps teens change from misbehavior to service. Through the power of group process, children and teens learn to change how they function in society.

Socializing Skills

Group therapy provides a safe group setting where group members can practice interpersonal skills; group-centered interventions provide a safe group setting where group members can practice school-based, classroom-oriented interpersonal skills. Dysfunctional interpersonal skills can lead to mental illness (Dweck, 2000). Children learn to interact with fellow classmates, to share, to take turns, to resolve conflicts without fighting, to be less competitive or judgmental of others, and to restructure learning patterns so they can do well in the classroom.

Modeling

There is always some imitation in group settings. Modeling is an essential part of rebuilding self-efficacy (Bandura, 1995). Children learn from watching other children in the group, and teenagers particularly learn from modeling for others in a group setting. Every group-centered intervention must include provisions to rebuild self-efficacy. Successful long-term change is not possible without rebuilding self-efficacy (Bandura, 1997).

Interpersonal Learning

The need to belong is a persistent and fundamental motivational need of all human beings (Baumeister & Leary, 1995). Personality develops across the life span, influenced by the interpersonal relationships and daily interactions of the individual (Kernis, 2003). Mental illness grows out of dysfunctional interpersonal relationships (Yalom & Leszcz, 2005). Therefore, school-based mental health must encompass learning how to interact in a healthy, positive, and constructive way.

Being told that you are behaving inappropriately or have not learned the textbook material being tested does not bring about change. Students must have a corrective experience in which they learn not only how to change, but also how to correct improper behavior. From a skills standpoint, they must learn to correct information from the classroom that they learned incorrectly. Interpersonally, group participants must learn how to interact in a positive way with others in a group. It is because they are interactive that groups make such a strong contribution to change.

Group Cohesion

For a group intervention to be successful, the group must be cohesive. Confrontational or competitive groups do not work for erasing academic failure. The group must be warm and accepting, understanding and supportive, safe, and cohesively constructive. Members must have a sense of belonging to the group; they must believe in the group and what the group does, and they must feel that the group accepts and appreciates their contribution to the group. It is a bonding process. Cohesion does not happen automatically. Cohesion must be built into every group intervention. Cohesion becomes even more vital with at-risk children or teens because they have not experienced peer acceptance from their classroom group. A cohesively structured group-centered intervention gives at-risk children and teens a chance to experience positive interaction and acceptance by peers.

Catharsis

The group setting allows students to express frustrations and fears, and to talk about problems, but group interventions go one step further than just expressing frustrations. Group-centered interventions help students resolve problems and erase fears. Creativity leads to wellness (Garai, 2001). Imaginative play and hands-on gluing projects help children alter their mood, relax, and give them release from anger and fear (Malchiodi, 2005).

Applying clown makeup and developing a clown personality helps teens learn to change. Through change in the group, teens learn to change their behavior outside of the group.

Returning to the Classroom

For a group-centered intervention to be effective, students must be able to take the new skills learned in the group back to their classroom. This includes acceptance that it is the student's responsibility to bring about this change.

Group interventions allow young people to learn how to change and then take their new knowledge or behaviors back to the classroom and use them effectively. Groups generate more opportunities for corrective experiences than do one-on-one tutoring or individual counseling (Fuhriman & Burlingame, 1994). The students must perceive the group to provide a safe and supportive environment in which they can work and interact and they must be able to rebuild self-efficacy before they can take what is learned and transfer it back to the classroom setting.

Group-centered interventions are both an emotional interactive experience and a group-centered corrective avenue for change. To be effective, group-centered interventions must be interactive in nature and must help the group work toward some form of corrective change that is needed to function effectively in their school-based setting. Purely fun experiences do not produce change; the group experience must incorporate skill building and efficacy retraining for the group intervention to succeed and to help children transfer their skills back to the class-room. The group becomes a social microcosm. Feedback from the group must be constructive. Interpersonal learning becomes the medium of change.

Groups for Children

Play is the natural communication of children (Landreth, 2002). Children express their feelings and problems more comfortably through play because play is part of a child's natural developmental learning process. Adding an atmosphere of play to group process involves creating a nurturing environment where children feel accepted and safe and are therefore willing to risk exploring tasks that may be difficult for them or at which they may have failed in the traditional classroom. The goal of effective group process is to help children resume normal development. This goal is met by helping children develop new pathways for learning material that they were not able to learn in the classroom.

A group atmosphere provides a motivational environment where children can learn, allowing children to work at mastery of a task at their own pace. A group-centered intervention can serve as a medium through which to practice social skills, teamwork, and group participation.

Learning and change occur by structuring the child's behaviors. Group-centered interventions accomplish this with action-oriented, hands-on learning centers, teamwork, and one-on-one remedial assistance. Group process helps children grow developmentally and learn more successfully. Offering challenging activities pushes children to work slightly above their present level of development, thus learning new skills and solving old problems. Through an atmosphere of play and intrinsic motivation, children can develop a more positive self-concept, assume a more active role and be more self-directive toward learning, be more accepting of their skills and abilities, experience a feeling of control, become more sensitive to the needs of others, and learn to cope with difficult situations without simply giving up (Landreth, 2002).

Group-centered interventions can be the difference between learning and failing. Play creates an atmosphere that builds a positive self-efficacy and helps children develop a sense of pride and a feeling of accomplishment. Combining group cohesion with intrinsic motivation encourages children to become self-directed and fully engaged in the classroom and for life.

Groups for Teenagers

Teenagers make decisions by observing others and by practicing or imitating behaviors that they see performed by others (Bandura, 1977). The structure of the group and the feedback from other adolescent participants in the group influence the interpersonal learning that takes place (Seligman, 1990). If the feedback from peers is positive, supportive, and skill building, then the interpersonal experiences of teen group members have a much greater chance of reducing alcohol and drug use, high-risk sexual behavior, anger, bullying, and violence (Catalano et al., 2003).

Social needs are not fully set during preadolescence (Dishion, Capaldi, & Yoerger, 1999). Adolescents acquire social needs through interactive social and environmental experiences and learning to interpret the perceptions of others (Dishion, McCord, & Poulin, 1999). Social needs influence adolescent behavior and decisions (Fischhoff et al., 2000).

Group involvement becomes a need-satisfying incentive if the group fulfills the thinking patterns, emotional feelings, or perceived behavior that adolescents believe will make them feel happy and accepted (Huebner & Mancini, 2003; Mahoney & Stattin, 2000). Involvement with a positive group can benefit a young person. Involvement with a negative group can be very destructive. Group participation and coping skills may be key factors in helping teenagers resist risky behaviors (George, Larson, Koenig, & McCullough, 2000).

Fuhriman and Burlingame (1990) stress that groups offer a unique advantage; group members have the opportunity to be both helpers and seekers of help. This is particularly important for teenagers, as they see others struggling with the same questions that they are facing. A group can provide members with a feeling of acceptance and of belonging to a community (Underwood & Teresi, 2002); members feel less isolated, and a group can provide a safe structure for interpersonal learning (Yalom and Leszcz, 2005).

The key, then, is to develop groups that offer children and teens an opportunity to grow and develop healthy behaviors. A healthy group must encourage positive self-efficacy, utilize intrinsic motivation rather than rewards and prizes, and fully emphasize and use the power of cohesive group process. The question that remains is how to shape group process.

Developing a Cohesive Group Format: A Case Study

The way that a group-centered intervention utilizes group process can have a direct effect on the group members' motivation and success. Let us return to our example of the Camp Sharigan motivational reading program.

In developing reading programs for children with poor reading skills, I tested three different group approaches with the same group of children to see which would be most effective. This was an inner-city group of first through third graders, and we used hands-on activities from Camp Sharigan that had proven to work so successfully at other locations.

First, we conducted an eleven-week program and worked with thirty children for one hour, once a week. The once-a-week format is frequently used in school-based settings. The program was held in one large room with separate tables for each group. The children wrote puppet play stories and made puppets. Puppets had proven to be a successful motivator at every site. In the once-a-week program, the children seemed to lose interest over the eleven-week period. They enjoyed making a puppet, but did not really care about writing their story or presenting their puppet play.

Next, we returned for an intensive one-day Saturday program. Thirty-nine children participated and worked in a school classroom format with individual tutors. Each child had a tutor, usually a teen or college student. The children became too competitive in the large classroom setting. There was no group cohesion or desire to work together and help each other.

For our third experience, we used the Camp Sharigan format of an intense week-long program for thirty children. We planned a four-day after-school program that met for two hours a day. The program emphasized learning centers, encouraging students to follow step-by-step directions, and used hands-on projects. Group cohesion and a high level of motivation were maintained all four days. One child arrived an hour before the reading clinic was scheduled to begin; his teacher was amazed. "He never reads unless you force him. He's sitting at the Rainbow Bridge reading a book, waiting until it's time to start. He doesn't even want to play a game on the computer; he just wants to read."

Group cohesion and motivation were high all four days because we were using group process and the power of group cohesion to create a group in which children worked together and supported one another. The same children who were fighting and arguing earlier in the classroom setting were now sitting down and helping one another.

Real-World Applications

Observational Extensions

Find a group of children or teens trying to make a decision on their own. This may be a decision about where to go for dinner or a decision about what game to play on the playground.

- How do the group members go about making a decision?
- Is everyone pleased with the decision?
- Did any of the group members leave the group because of the decision?

A Ready-to-Use Group-Centered Intervention: "Down at the Pizza Shop"

This is an excellent group-centered intervention for children or teens. It is a wonderful way to encourage students to work together in groups. For students who struggle with cooperative learning projects or with working in groups, this intervention encourages even the most reluctant group member to participate.

Objective: To build group process through encouraging children or teens to share their ideas, fears, and feelings.

Time: 1 hour (Can be expanded if desired).

Supplies: paper, markers, and scissors

1. Say to the group, "Today, we are a pizza shop and, just like pizza shops around town, we want to make the best pizza in the shortest amount of time so that we can bring in the most customers."

2. Have paper available for the crust, sauce, cheese, ground beef, sausage, pepperoni, green peppers, mushrooms, olives, and anchovies—a total of ten layers to put together.

3. Answer the questions as you put each layer of the pizza together. They may not leave out a layer, and each person in the group must provide an answer to every question.

4. Start with layer 1, the crust: "What is the most important decision you will ever have to make in life? Write your answers on a large paper circle for the crust." Go to the next layer, which is the sauce.

5. Sauce: Ask each group member to write down something they would like to change about their life. Have each person write down a suggestion on the paper circle. Tell them to cut around the circle and place the paper sauce layer on top of their crust. Then, they add the next layer, which is the cheese.

6. Cheese: "Write down six service projects we could do together as a group to help other people in our community or around the world. Write on a circle of cheese. Cut around the circle and place the paper cheese layer on top of your sauce. Go and get the next layer, the ground beef."

7. Ground Beef: "Write down six different things we could do to become a closer group of friends and a more supportive group." Have each person write their suggestion on this paper circle. "Cut around the circle and place the paper ground beef layer on top of your cheese. Go and get the next topping, which is sausage."

8. Sausage: Cut out pieces of round sausage. Have the group members write down something they enjoy doing with others in a group. "Place each piece of sausage on top of the ground beef layer. Go and get the pepperoni."

9. Pepperoni: Cut out pieces of pepperoni. Ask each person to write down a different problem they think students face at school or at home. "Write your answers on the pepperoni circles. Place each piece of pepperoni on top of the ground beef layer. The next topping will be green peppers."

10. Green Peppers: Cut out green pepper slices. Have each person write down a different problem at their school. Write each problem on a separate circle. Arrange the green pepper slices on top of the pizza. The next topping will be mushrooms.

11. Mushrooms: Cut out mushroom slices. Have each person write down an idea for being kinder to others. Arrange mushrooms on top of the pizza. Now, put on the olives.

12. Olives: Cut out olives. Have each person write down something he or she worries about. Write each idea on a separate olive. Arrange olives on top of the pizza. The last topping will be the anchovies.

13. Anchovies: Cut out anchovies. Arrange anchovies on top of the pizza. Have each person write down a way to get help when you worry. Discuss ways to help each other as a group.

    Plan a project to do together as a group. It can be a project to help others or an activity to strengthen friendships within the group.

5
Selecting Effective Interventions

A ten-foot-high chain link fence with barbed wire stretched across the top greeted us as we parked beside the playground. The playground was concrete and gravel. A rusty basketball hoop sagged from a pole in the center of the playground. The remains of a swing set sat empty without swings. There was a huge padlock on the gate. We were not in prison; we were at an elementary school. The bars covering the windows of the school characterized the atmosphere in which these children worked and played. The goal was to work with thirty first through sixth grade students who had been removed from the public school for discipline violations. The group-centered intervention was to be three hours a day for five days. An eighteen-year-old sixth grader in the group was still reading at the first grade reading level. Many of the students said that they never opened a book or read during the summer. Some even said that they did not have books to read at home and never went to the library. As one young man explained, "I get everything I need off the TV."

Every child has the ability to learn, but not every child can learn in the same structured classroom setting. There does not have to be an achievement gap or academic failure; we can become a society blessed with academic success and mental well-being. Our nation's mental health depends on how we handle children who struggle to learn in the classroom. An effective prevention program can change a child's life forever.

The question then arises: How do we identify an effective prevention program in school-based settings? Let us return to our three theoretical principles. For a group intervention to erase classroom failure, it must (1) rebuild self-efficacy, (2) rely on intrinsic motivation, and (3) fully employ the therapeutic power of cohesive group process. Although many group interventions have proven over time to be successful in treating trauma, anxiety, depression, eating disorders, and other forms of dysfunctional behavior, we will limit our discussion to classroom-based academic failure. We will compare six of the most frequently used school-based group therapies—expressive therapies, brief small group counseling, short-term play therapy, academic counseling, developmental therapy, and cognitive behavioral interventions—to the three theoretical principles cited above.

E. Clanton Harpine, *Group Interventions in Schools.*
© Springer Science + Business Media, LLC 2008

1. *Expressive therapies:* Expressive therapies rely on intrinsic motivation. Writing, drawing, and painting all lead to creative self-expression and help to energize and redirect feelings of frustration and anxiety. Art and music are wonderful ways to enhance relaxation and alter mood (Malchiodi, 2005). Creativity can promote wellness (Garai, 2001), but expressive therapies alone do not provide the skill-building activities necessary to rebuild self-efficacy. As Albert Bandura (1995) warns, unless one gives children the skills needed to be successful in the classroom, failure will quickly return. Expressive therapies seem to be more frequently found in individual, one-on-one therapy rather than in group therapy, although expressive therapies are sometimes used in group settings to foster self-expression and acceptance (Malchiodi, 2005). Therefore, we do not see extensive use of group process in expressive therapies. Art and music are excellent media for encouraging intrinsic motivation and are very successful in redirecting and refocusing unwanted behavior, as many of the examples cited throughout this book demonstrate, but intrinsic motivation alone is not enough. Children who fail in the classroom need skill-building as well as therapy. Group-centered interventions build on the concept of expressive therapies and add self-efficacy and cohesive group process.

2. *Brief small-group counseling:* Another counseling technique frequently used in school-based settings is brief small-group counseling. As the term implies, brief counseling is time-limited, possibly six or eight sessions. Brief counseling is usually action-based. Action-based counseling ranges from suggesting that a student try a particular action or solution (Sink, 2005) to hands-on action-oriented group sessions as with the Camp Sharigan program. Brief, small-group counseling can be quite effective if it includes self-efficacy retraining and intrinsically motivating activities, while fully utilizing the therapeutic power of cohesive group process. If, however, the group is a collective setting for the individual counseling of students, where counselors merely go around the circle asking the students to explain their problem or feelings in turn (Jacobs & Schimmel, 2005), then brief small-group counseling is likely to fail with students suffering from academic failure. In such situations, there is no rebuilding of self-efficacy and there is no intrinsic motivation; nor does a mere circle use group process or cohesion. Although individual short-term therapy may be effective for other needs, it does not answer the needs of children struggling in the classroom unless it rebuilds self-efficacy, stresses intrinsic motivation, and builds a cohesive group for children to work in. Without these three principles, there is no change in academic failure and there is no effective group counseling taking place (Arrow, 2005). For group counseling to be effective, the group must be interactive (Burlingame, Fuhriman, & Johnson, 2004).

3. *Short-term play therapy:* Another form of time-limited therapy often found in school-based settings with children and teenagers is short-term play therapy. As the term implies, there is a limited time frame or a preset therapy schedule (Kaduson & Schaefer, 2006). Short-term play therapy is frequently used in school-based settings for disruptive behavior that can stem from academic failure and feelings of inadequacy. Games and play techniques can help children focus on

their problem, but the intrinsic self-expression of play does not always transfer back to the classroom with children who suffer from academic failure. Most short-term play therapy interventions stress a reward system to encourage compliance once the child returns to the classroom (Riviere, 2006). Reward systems are extrinsic. As emphasized earlier, rewards do not help children learn to change (Deci & Ryan, 1985). Short-term play therapy also does not include a technique for rebuilding self-efficacy, although some short-term play therapy interventions do stress self-esteem (Riviere, 2006). As noted in Chapter 2, it is self-efficacy that is essential for academic improvement, not self-esteem (Bandura, 1995). A child or teenager may have high self-esteem and still be a failure in the classroom (Marmarosh et al., 2005). Skill-building is essential (Bandura, 1997). Short-term play therapy does not teach academic skills; therefore, children return to the classroom still unable to read, spell, or add. Continued failure triggers continued disruptive behavior.

As for group process, most short-term play therapy is individual one-on-one therapy, but group play therapy is useful for active instruction, such as with role plays, supervised practice of appropriate behavior, corrective feedback or prompting, and independent homework practice (Blundon & Schaefer, 2006). Although these may be effective direct instruction techniques, they do not build cohesion in the group or engage the therapeutic power of group process, for the group does not function as a group. Children are merely assembled for the purpose of instruction. For group process to be effective, children and teens must function as a group to learn to solve problems together. Without interaction, there is no group process (Yalom & Leszcz, 2005). The therapeutic power of groups helps to bring about academic and behavioral change. Although short-term play therapy may be effective for other classroom problems, a child experiencing academic failure will still feel inadequate in the classroom and will still be disruptive.

4. *Academic counseling:* Academic counseling, as the term implies, focuses on academic problems in the classroom. Attention-deficit hyperactivity disorder (ADHD) is a primary area of concern in the classroom and particularly with academic counseling (Parsons, 2006). Most academic counseling interventions used in school-based settings for ADHD center on training parents, training classroom teachers, or training students to monitor their behavior (Parsons, 2006). The same is true for children getting up out of their seat, daydreaming, and not turning in homework.

Most teachers and counselors using academic counseling techniques rely on goal setting and extrinsic reward and consequence systems to keep students on-task in the classroom (Parsons, 2006). Academic counseling as it is used in most school-based settings does not emphasize rebuilding self-efficacy and does not employ intrinsic motivation, or stress group cohesion (Parsons, 2006). Although goal-setting contributes to self-efficacy, goal setting alone is not enough to rebuild self-efficacy (Bandura & Cervone, 2000). Consequently, children meet with only modest success or improve for only a short period of time (DuPaul, Vile Junod, & Flammer, 2006). Extrinsic rewards may tempt children to comply temporarily, but they do not bring about long-term change or help them rebuild positive self-efficacy (Henderlong & Lepper, 2002).

As long as academic counseling (Parsons, 2006) is tied to extrinsic reward systems, it cannot be successful in school-based settings (Ryan & Deci, 2000) with ADHD, academic failure, disruptive classroom behavior, or violence, aggression, and bullying. To be effective, academic counseling must rebuild self-efficacy (Bandura, 1997), use intrinsic motivators, and rely on the change-inducing power of cohesive group process.

5. *Cognitive-behavioral therapy:* Cognitive-behavioral therapy is used in school-based settings for a multitude of problems. Cognitive-behavioral therapy strives to assist students with the acquisition of new skills, both cognitive and behavioral, by structuring sessions to bring about a change in how students cognitively process and think (Mennuti, Freeman, & Christner, 2006). Cognitive-behavioral therapists focus on changing the student's belief system. Cognitive-behavioral therapy has succeeded with anxiety disorders and social phobias (Gosch & Flannery-Schroeder, 2006), but has not been as successful with academic failure (DuPaul et al., 2006; Kearney, Lemos, & Silverman, 2006). Cognitive-behavioral therapy is primarily an individual therapy approach, but has been used in groups for children and teens who are being treated for depression (Donoghue, Wheeler, Prout, Wilson, & Reinecke, 2006). In Donoghue et al.'s approach, group interventions are described as direct instruction, modeling, homework assignments, relaxation, and developing skills. There is no group building or cohesion; the group is simply used as an instructional setting for teaching individual skills.

6. *Developmental therapy:* In contrast, Schneider Corey and Corey (2006) describe using a developmental group approach with students in a school-based setting with a relaxed structure. Developmental groups are designed for support and to teach coping skills for the classroom (Kram Laudenslager, 2006). Group techniques include reading stories, going around the circle and having the children report how they feel, focusing on one child at a time, providing an anonymous question box for difficult questions the child does not want to ask out loud, listening games, and even making collages (Christenson, 2006; Kram Laudenslager, 2006; Schneider Corey & Corey, 2006). Developmental groups seem mostly to be discussion groups for depression, anger management, and other emotional problems. This approach uses group process, but the authors do not mention intrinsic motivation or self-efficacy. Even Hans Steiner (2004), who gives us a comprehensive practical guide for using developmental psychology for mental health interventions, stops short of offering in-depth interventions for school-based settings. Thus, these programs do not undertake to accomplish the same goals as group-centered interventions.

Comparing these six popular school-based approaches to our three theoretical principles for effective preventative programs in academic failure, none of the six fulfills the requirements outlined by Albert Bandura (1995) for rebuilding self-efficacy, considered to be essential for erasing academic failure (Bandura, 1977; Multon et al. 1991; Schunk, 1991). All but expressive therapies (Malchiodi, 2005) and possibly developmental interventions rely on extrinsic reward systems. Even advocates of play-therapy (Riviere, 2006) and cognitive-behavioral interventions often talk about tokens and rewards (Mennuti et al., 2006). Very few school-based programs use group interventions, and those that do use groups chiefly as a setting for direct instruction (Blundon & Schaefer, 2006; Donoghue et al., 2006; Jacobs & Schimmel, 2005; Parsons, 2006). Except with developmental group interventions, there is no development of group cohesion; thus, there is no group process. The group is a vehicle for small group classroom instruction. All of these different kinds of programs and therapies can be useful, but they do not accomplish the same purposes as group-centered interventions. Therefore, when counselors, psychologists, and school-based mental health practitioners seek to find group interventions that actually help children erase the perception of failure and return to the classroom ready to learn, we need to seek group interventions that rebuild self-efficacy, use intrinsic motivation, and build cohesive group process. What we need are group interventions that transform failure into success today and tomorrow.

Purely educational programs are also not designed to accomplish the same purposes as therapeutic group interventions. Robert Slavin and Nancy Madden (2001) describe and compare their Success for All program with the Reading Recovery program. These two very popular programs, used in public schools to reduce classroom failure, enjoy academic success with first graders, but their success seems to trail off by the second and third grade (Slavin & Madden, 2001). If we compare such programs to our three principles for effective group interventions—self-efficacy, intrinsic motivation, and cohesive group process—we note that there is no rebuilding of self-efficacy, no intrinsic motivation, and no group process. Both programs are one-on-one tutoring programs, which the National Reading Panel (2000) found to be less effective than group approaches. They are strictly educational programs and do not rebuild self-efficacy.

Group-centered interventions combine self-efficacy, intrinsic motivation, and cohesive group process to create a group intervention that erases classroom failure. If we are to develop successful group interventions, we must fit our interventions to the needs of the child or teenager experiencing academic failure. Group-centered interventions help children correct learning deficiencies before they lead to behavioral and mental health problems.

Identifying the Needs of the Client

An example from the Camp Sharigan program illustrates the necessity of fitting the intervention to the needs of the child. A school-based after-school program placed a young third-grader in my Camp Sharigan group intervention because he had been labeled by the school as having attention-deficit disorder (ADD) and identified as having trouble staying on task in the classroom. As a result, his academic progress was suffering. The child had a great deal of difficulty the first day at Camp Sharigan and even broke down in tears twice. I worked one-on-one with him and immediately began to suspect that his problems were much deeper than mere academic failure. After his difficulty on the first day, he completed the Camp Sharigan program successfully, returned to the classroom, and improved academically.

Next, the after-school program placed him in a short-term play therapy group organized to reduce fights on the school bus and improve interaction among students. Again, he struggled to work in a group setting. He would get up and walk away from the play therapy group session and had to be returned by staff. It was not until the end of the six short-term sessions that he began to participate in the play therapy group. I began to observe him on the playground. He did not participate in games; did not talk with or interact with other children, only with adults; and spent most of his time clinging to the playground's chain-link fence. His academic work had improved after Camp Sharigan and he stopped fighting on the school bus, but there was still an as-yet-unresolved problem.

In such situations, students may need individual one-on-one counseling before being placed in group therapy. Again, there is never one single answer or intervention that is best for every child or every problem.

Sometimes academic problems in the classroom stem from problems other than academic failure. Death of a parent, domestic violence, or even a life-threatening illness may be the underlying cause of low reading comprehension or failure to read at grade level (Boyd Webb, 1999). In such instances, neither skill building nor efficacy retraining will correct the problem. Crisis intervention and assessment may be needed. Joyce Bluestone (1999) describes just such a situation in a case study of a fifth-grade girl experiencing reading comprehension problems. Crisis play therapy intervention through puppetry and the formation of a peer therapy dyad helped the child cope and adjust to the unexpected death of her father (Bluestone, 1999). Coping with this crisis in her life then enabled her to continue successfully in school.

Counselors and other mental health practitioners working in school-based settings must fit the group intervention to the needs of the students. No one group intervention can fit every need.

Real-World Applications

Observational Extensions

Observe children in the classroom after various types of group interventions. List the advantages and disadvantages that you see for each intervention in terms of behavior that transfers back to the classroom.

A Ready-to-Use Group-Centered Intervention: "Helping Others"

I find that one of the best ways to help children place perspective on their own problems is through story writing. A story can often initiate discussion within a group. Working on a story together as a group also helps to build group cohesion.

This particular group-centered intervention raises many questions for discussion on problems common to most classrooms.

Stories help children work on reading and comprehension skills. The story pays extra attention to detail so that you can review and stress details from the story with the students. Story writing encourages children to pay attention to the details in a story so that they will be able to write an ending to the story or tell what happens next. This is a group-centered intervention that can be used for one session or for three sessions. Use the stories as separate chapters and review to enhance comprehension.

Objective: To motivate students to work on comprehension skills and to encourage discussion of classroom problems.
Time: Can be used for a 1-hour session or for three sessions.
Supplies needed: Pencils and paper for students.

Read the following story to the students or have the children take turns reading the story to the group.

Session 1: "The Worst Day in History"

It was one of the worst days I could ever remember. There were four fourth-grade classes, and the four of us had been placed in separate classes. How could they do this to us? We had been best of friends since our sandbox days.

Sing-Sing, Loella, Anna, and I all moved to Cedar Hill Drive on the cul-de-sac in the still unfinished new housing development at the edge of town when we were four years old. Our parents had been transferred here to work in the new plastics factory.

The housing development was built by the factory, but still sat unfinished because the development had run out of money when the plant shut down and many of the workers were laid off. Sing-Sing, Loella, Anna, and I were the only kids living on our street; so of course we had to be friends.

Through kindergarten, first, second, and third grade, they had allowed at least two of us to stay together in the same class. Now, we were all split up. The principal said it was something about "allowing us to make new friends and enrich our personalities."

No matter what, we promised to stay best of friends forever. We'd keep that promise too, through thick and through thin.

When allowed, we ate lunch together. When not, we sat across the cafeteria from each other and mouthed comments back and forth.

Not a one of us would have ever given one ounce of thought to going off and playing with someone else. We were a foursome.

We walked to and from school together. We did homework together. We gossiped about who we did and didn't like every single day after school. We even cried over tests together. We were the inseparable, unlikeliest foursome you could ever imagine.

Sing-Sing was from China. Every time anyone said her name, they immediately thought of the panda bear in the Washington Zoo. Sing-Sing hated being named after a panda bear.

The teachers at school decided to call Sing-Sing Sally, to help her Americanize herself. We refused. To us, she was Sing-Sing.

Loella's father was from Puerto Rico, although Loella had been born here in the States. Loella was named after her grandmother, but absolutely no one could pronounce her name correctly.

Loella and Sing-Sing had moved to Cedar Hill Drive the exact same day I had. Our moving vans arrived within hours of each other.

My little sister Carey was only six months old back then and not much fun to play with. Sing-Sing was an only child. Loella had four older brothers. So the three of us did everything together.

My dad built us a big sandbox and a tree house. Loella had a gigantic swing set, slide, and horse glider. Sing-Sing had a tire swing.

Sing-Sing's swing was made from a huge tractor tire. There was room for all of us on the tire swing together. We loved to twist the chain as tight as we could and then spin till we were so dizzy we staggered when we walked.

My tree house was our secret hideout. No boys allowed.

Our days were filled with continuous fun. We played back and forth between our adjoining yards as if it was one big playground.

Three months later, Anna and her little brother Horace moved to Cedar Hill Drive. Anna, whose father called her by her full name, Annastashia, was vice president of something at the plant.

Two months after Anna and her family moved in, the factory shut down for six months, so none of the other houses that were planned for our street were ever built. Anna didn't want to get stuck playing with her little brother; so naturally she played with us.

We never argued, we never fought, and we never invited other friends over. It was always just the four of us.

Now the school had done the unthinkable, they had separated us. Sing-Sing and Anna were the bravest; they had already gone into their new classrooms.

Loella stood looking at me from down the hall. She shrugged her shoulders, turned, and walked through the doorway.

I was the only one left. I stood breathing fast with my hand poised slightly above the doorknob.

I was ready to turn the knob and go inside, but my hand just wouldn't move. No matter how hard I tried I couldn't make my fingers grasp hold of the doorknob. I could see my fingers trembling.

What was I afraid of? What was the worst that could happen?

Discussion with the Children

"You're the authors. What is Kristina afraid of? What do you think is the worst thing that could happen? What do you think will happen next?"

Session 2: "Nancy Allison"

I could be stuck in class with Nancy Allison. That's what could happen.

Nancy's father was president of the factory where my dad worked. She was the biggest snob I had ever seen. She hated me, and I hated her.

Nancy loved to tease me about my homemade clothes and the way I dressed. It wasn't that we were poor. We didn't have as much money as Nancy's family, but then, no one did.

My dad was a cost accountant and made a good living. There was enough money to go to the store and buy clothes like other normal people, but my mother thought she was being sweet by making my sister and me homemade skirts and dresses. She wasn't.

Mother always said, "By making your clothes instead of just buying you something off the rack, I'm showing you how special you are to me. I make each outfit with love just for you."

It wasn't that she wasn't a good seamstress, because she was; and I actually kind of liked the neat kitty cat quilted skirt and other outfits she made for me, but mother just didn't understand that kids don't dress like that at school. Mother lived in her own little dream world of how life should be, not how it actually was. Mother would go around saying, "Well, if that's not how things are, then it's up to you to change them."

Mother was an old 1960s "change the world do-gooder" who never grew up. She went around playing Peter, Paul, and Mary tapes and saying, "What these kids need today is music with a message." Mom boycotts Nestlé and Exxon, even though, I think she has long since forgotten why, and continues to harp on the evils of the Vietnam War as if it were still going on today. Mother simply didn't understand that times had changed.

Or had they? Here I was about to walk into my new schoolroom wearing a homemade skirt with puppy dogs all over it. Some even had little red tongues hanging out of their mouths.

It was actually a cute skirt, but this is fourth grade, and I'm too old for homemade clothes. My white lace trimmed anklets were the worst though.

I tried to tell Mom that none of the girls wore lacy socks to school anymore, but Mom just said, "That's nonsense! They're so cute on you. Don't be in such a hurry to grow up."

If the skirt and socks were not enough, my blouse was one of those children's brands that little kids wear. It had a round Peter Pan lace-trimmed collar. I hated the thought of listening to the other girls teasing me all day.

At least I had three friends in the world. Sing-Sing, Anna, and Loella never teased me about my clothes.

Rin-n-n-ng!

Now, on top of everything else, I was late. With trembling hands, I bravely reached for the doorknob, pulled the door toward me with a slight jerk, and walked inside. There she sat, my worst nightmare, in a brand-new slinky silver gray slightly low cut dress that barely covered what it needed to on either end with matching stockings and clogs. Nancy Allison was definitely the epitome of the fashion scene and undoubtedly going to be the main source of my trouble throughout fourth grade.

"Welcome, Kristie! I'm so glad you're in my class this year," said Mr. Jordan.

At least I had gotten the nicest of the fourth grade teachers for homeroom.

"Why don't you take a seat right here at the front next to Nancy," continued Mr. Jordan, as he motioned to a desk at the front of the room beside Nancy Allison.

Nothing could be worse. This year was definitely doomed. I'll never survive.

I was totally mortified to see that the only empty desk remaining in the entire classroom was at the very front of the room, squarely positioned directly in line with Mr. Jordan's desk and naturally right next to Nancy Allison. Today would be recorded on the pages of history books as the worst day ever at Carmelton Elementary.

Discussion with the Children

"You're the authors. What will Nancy do? What will happen to Kristie? Have you ever had a problem with another student in your class? What did you do?"

Session 3:   "Chewing Gum And More"

"Oh, Mr. Jordan, you can't be serious. Kristie can't possibly sit here. Judy's moving up." Nancy quickly motioned to Judy in the back row to hurry and scoot into the vacant desk.

Unfortunately for me, Judy didn't move as fast as Mr. Jordan spoke.

"Judy's fine where she is. Kristie, take your seat."

I did as I was told.

Nancy spun around in her chair with a "Humph!"

It wasn't my fault. I didn't want to sit next to Nancy Allison any more than Nancy wanted to be stuck with me.

I was the only African-American girl in class. As a matter of fact we were the only African-American family in Carmelton.

As I said, I'd never really thought much about it. Sing-Sing, Loella, and Anna never seemed to notice, but Nancy Allison did.

Nancy always crossed to the other side of the hallway when I walked by. She would announce at the top of her lungs that I wasn't allowed to sit at her lunch table. And she did everything in her power to make it perfectly clear that she considered herself to be far superior to me.

Being dumped into the same class as Nancy Allison was the worst possible thing that could have happened to me, except maybe being forced to sit right next to her.

"Mr. Jordan, it's stuffy in here. May we open a window?" Nancy waved her hand to fan herself.

Nancy turned sideways in her chair. Crossed her legs and fluffed her hair.

"The air conditioning is on, Nancy. You'll be fine," Mr. Jordan replied.

I slammed my notebook down onto my desk and glared at Nancy. She smiled and turned back to face Mr. Jordan in triumph.

"Let's take the lunch count. Buyers stand up. Packers stay seated." Mr. Jordan counted out loud as he pointed with his pencil up and down each row. "That can't be right, folks. Let's do it again. The lunch count shouldn't take all day. By the time you get to fourth grade, you know whether you're going to buy your lunch or whether you packed a lunch this morning and brought it from home."

It took three or four tries before Mr. Jordan was satisfied that he had everyone accounted for. Nancy, of course, was buying her lunch and stood up with a giggle each time Mr. Jordan had to recount.

Mr. Jordan had made name tags for all of our desks. We had to color in the loops that were formed by writing our names in cursive letters. It was sort of neat how Mr. Jordan had created a mirror effect by writing our names one on top of the other.

Next, Mr. Jordan told us to draw a picture at the end of our name. I hate it when teachers ask you to draw pictures that describe you as a person or demand that you stand up and tell something about yourself.

So, naturally, our next task was to stand up and show everyone our picture and name tag. Was it possible for this day to get any worse? Little did I know, but the answer's always YES.

Nancy stood up when it was her turn and said, "My name's Nancy Allison. My father is the president and CEO of the Carmelton Plastics Factory. My mother is president of the PTO here at school, and on the hospital board, and active at the country club." Nancy gave an appropriate giggle as if we should all be impressed. "I drew a picture of my house. See?"

Nancy waved her name tag back and forth. She had drawn a picture of an enormous mansion with a circle drive out front.

It's true that her house was big, but I think the picture made it look even worse than it was.

"Now, it's your turn, Kristie," she announced. "What did you draw?"

I stood and announced that my name was Kristina McCormick, as it said on my name tag, and said, "This is my dog, Skipper."

"Skipper," Nancy squealed. "What a funny name for a dog." The entire class joined Nancy in a loud round of laughter.

"Can you tell us why your dog's named Skipper, Kristine?"

I know that Mr. Jordan was trying to be nice, but he only made matters worse.

"My name's Kristina, with an A, not an E."

The entire class roared. I was so embarrassed.

"I apologize, Kristina. Please continue."

"Oh yes, do tell us, why on earth did you name your dog, Skipper?" Nancy reclaimed center stage.

Nancy Allison had no intention of letting Mr. Jordan ruin her moment of triumph over me. She had succeeded in making a fool of me and she enjoyed every second of it.

"I go by Kristie."

"I'll try to remember that," Mr. Jordan promised.

"I don't know why we named my dog, Skipper. We just did." The room filled with laughter a third time at my expense.

"Well, I think Skipper is an excellent name for a dog, and that's a fine drawing, Kristie, thank you." Mr. Jordan smiled and motioned for me to be seated.

As I looked around the room, there was not one friendly face. I knew most of the kids, and they knew me, but the class was mostly filled with Nancy's friends. How did they manage to all get in the same class together when we had to be split up? Sometimes adults don't seem fair.

Our next task of the morning was a math placement test. Maybe I'd flunk and have to be moved to a different classroom.

Math was not my strongest subject. Anna was a whiz at math. Reading was my specialty.

Evidently math wasn't Nancy's best subject either. We ended up in the same math and reading group. Fourth grade was definitely going to be the worst year of my life.

Our last task before lunch proved to be the final killer. We were making an "All About Me" booklet.

We were to bring a picture from home. Mr. Jordan also announced that each day we'd work in our "All About Me" booklets for an hour before lunch. After lunch and recess, we'd share what we wrote in our booklets.

The booklet had all sorts of questions like, "What's your favorite color, food …" that sort of thing. Then there were blank pages to write in "The Best Gift You Ever Received," "My Favorite Experience with My Mom or Dad," and naturally "What Do You Want to be When You Grow Up." The worst yet, though, was, "If I had three wishes, I'd wish for …"

No! How could Mr. Jordan do this to me?

First, I get stuck being in class with Nancy. Then Mr. Jordan cinches my fate by forcing us all to sit and listen to Nancy gloat every day about how wonderful she is and tell us over and over about how much money her father has. "All About Me" was going to be nothing but trouble.

Before I could give further thought to the disaster that Mr. Jordan had flung me into, the bell rang for lunch. I sprang out of my seat and dashed for the door. I couldn't wait to see Sing-Sing, Loella, and Anna.

I charged for the door but stopped short in front of my locker. Someone had smeared chewing gum all over my locker door. The handle and combination lock were covered in big wads of chewing gum.

I stood paralyzed, my hand in midair ready to reach for my locker handle, my mouth gaping open. A crowd gathered behind me.

"Mr. Jordan! Look at Kristine's locker," Nancy shouted at the top of her lungs.

Nancy knew perfectly well that my name was not Kristine, and she wanted to make sure everyone knew about my locker.

"It's awful! It's on the lock and everything. How will you ever get all the gum off, Kristine? Ooh! That's nasty!" Nancy proudly broadcast the state of my locker loud enough for the entire school to hear.

"On to lunch, everyone." Mr. Jordan dispersed the crowd. "Kristie, you might as well go on to lunch too."

"I can't. My lunch is in there." I pointed to my locker.

Tiny teardrops began to drip from the corners of my eyes. In fourth grade, you were considered a baby if you cried, but I couldn't help it.

Mr. Jordan ushered me back into the classroom. I put my head down on my desk to hide my face. Mr. Jordan pulled his chair over.

"I'm sorry, Kristie. I'll get the custodian to clean your locker."

I didn't respond.

Mr. Jordan talked on and on about how unfair other students could be. He was trying to be nice, but he succeeded only in making me feel worse.

He finally sent me on to lunch with a note saying I was allowed to charge my lunch today. I went to lunch but didn't go near the lunch line. I didn't feel like eating, and besides, I hated the food in the cafeteria. Even Skipper wouldn't have eaten from our school cafeteria.

Loella, Sing-Sing, and Anna saved me a seat over in the far corner. Every eye turned toward me as I entered the room. Silence penetrated every crevice of the cafeteria. Even the lunch monitors stood quietly by as I crossed the room.

"What happened?" Sing-Sing whispered before I even had a chance to sit down.

The normal lunchroom buzz of the cafeteria resumed. Several kids looked in my direction and pointed.

Did the entire school know about the chewing gum on my locker?

It seemed so.

"I don't know," I finally mumbled as I ducked my head and stared at the table.

"Where's your lunch?" Anna inquired.

"In my locker."

"Here, help me eat mine," Anna insisted.

She began piling food in front of me.

"My mother packs enough lunch for ten people," said Anna. "I have two sandwiches, an apple, grapes, yogurt, cookies, chips, and two drink boxes. That's in case I'm extra thirsty."

We all began to laugh. Sing-Sing donated half her donut. Loella gave me her box of raisins. Before long, we were trading food back and forth, sharing and swapping bites of everything.

It felt so wonderful to be back in our foursome again. At least the teachers hadn't ruined lunch and split us up by classes like last year.

During recess, the four of us went and hid up on the hill. There was a big pine tree. We liked to crawl inside beneath the low hanging branches and hide. It was sort of our secret hideout.

"How's your class?" I asked Loella.

"Okay, I guess. I have Miss Baker. She jumps around all over the room and screams and yells, but I sit in the back and ignore her. Max and Jason are both in my class."

We all groaned. Max and Jason were class clowns.

"It's not so bad," Loella said, "Max and Jason keep Miss Baker so busy telling them to sit down and behave that she doesn't have time to even notice I exist."

"I stuck a paperback inside my math book and read all morning," said Sing-Sing.

"It took Mrs. Johnson all morning just to call the roll. She gave us two whole pages of math to do, but I finished early so I read."

"She didn't catch you?" Loella inquired.

"No, she never even noticed," smiled Sing-Sing.

"You got stuck with Mr. Walerston, didn't you?" I asked Anna.

"Yes and he's as awful as everyone said," Anna replied.

"Does he really look like a walrus when he talks?" Sing-Sing asked, teasing.

"Worse, he bellows," said Anna.

We all laughed. It felt so wonderful to be among friends.

"Yours sounds worse, though, Kristie," Anna said.

"Nothing could be as bad as being in class with Nancy Allison, unless it's sitting right next to Nancy Allison, or being in the same math group and the same reading group as Nancy Allison. Trust me, nothing could be worse than Nancy."

"How's Mr. Jordan?" Loella asked.

"He's supposed to be nice," Anna offered.

"At least you got the best teacher," Sing-Sing announced.

"He's nice enough. He tries, but Nancy runs circles around him. Even when she's being hateful, he thinks she's trying to be nice. She's the biggest flirt I've ever seen too. She sits right in front of Mr. Jordan's desk. He thinks she's wonderful. 'Nancy, would you collect the papers. Nancy, put the lunch count on the outside of the door. Nancy, do you know the answer?' I'm sick and tired of Nancy, and it's still the first day."

"What are you going to do about your locker?" Sing-Sing asked the subject we were all avoiding.

"Mr. Jordan said he'd have the custodian clean the gum off."

"We have to figure out who did this," Loella snapped.

"How?" Anna asked.

"I'm not sure, but she's right," I mumbled. "We have to do something. It's getting worse."

"We have to stand up to them. You certainly can't count on the teachers to help," said Sing-Sing.

"They'll never figure out who did it. They'll just say it was an accident," I mumbled.

"How could it be an accident?" challenged Loella.

"Gum simply cannot smear itself all over a locker like that. I saw it. It was awful," Anna said with anger.

"We have to stand together," said Sing-Sing.

"Maybe that's not such a good idea," I cautioned.

"And why not?" Loella snapped.

"They might start harassing you too," I reminded my friends.

"We're a foursome. All for one," Anna smiled. "And don't you forget it, Kristie."

Discussion with the Children

"You're the authors. What will the girls do next? Who do you think was responsible for the chewing gum? Have you ever been teased or been the victim of a bad joke?"

6
A One-Week Group-Centered Motivational Intervention Program

I looked up and saw a little boy standing in the doorway as I arranged books on the rainbow bridge. When I asked if he would like to read a book, his brown eyes glowed and his smile stretched from ear to ear. As he made his selection and joined me on the bridge, he eagerly turned to the first page and began to read. At the end of the second sentence, he encountered a word that he did not know. Slamming the book shut, he said, "I can't read." His head sagged; his eyes starred blankly at the floor. No amount of persuasion convinced him to try again. By the end of the week, the same little boy came hurrying across the room waving a book and asking if I had time to listen to him read. As he proudly tackled even the hard words he didn't know, I thought, what a difference a week can make.

Learning to read occurs during such a sensitive period of childhood development that reading can then go on to affect us across our entire life span. If children learn to read in first grade, then reading becomes a very positive part of their life. If children are labeled as failures, at-risk of failing, or as slow readers, then reading can become the catalyst that leads to many school-based mental health problems (Oldfather, 2002).

Visit a nursing home; ask the residents if they remember their reading group in first or second grade. Eighty- and ninety-year-old seniors can still quickly tell you whether they were slow readers or one of the smart readers in their first grade class. Learning to read is so closely attached to our self-concept that it becomes a part of our identity (Deci et al., 1991). Therefore, the problem of reading failure must be solved. This is more than just a problem for the classroom teacher. Children's reading failure permeates all of their life, and thus it must be a primary concern of school counselors, psychologists, and, indeed, all mental health practitioners.

Reading failure is like the domino effect. Once a child falls behind, failure in reading begins to seep into every crevice of the educational process. Poor readers struggle to write, cannot read their social studies or science text, have difficulty with story problems in math, and do not volunteer to participate in any activities that require reading. Research has also shown a direct correlation between failure to read and dropping out of school, poor employment, and crime (Snowden, 2005; Twenge & Campbell, 2002).

E. Clanton Harpine, *Group Interventions in Schools.*
© Springer Science+Business Media, LLC 2008

Children who fail to learn to read in school are often kept back a grade, which increases the likelihood that a student will drop out of school before graduation (Nastasi et al., 2004; Orfield & Lee, 2005). Aggressive behavior, depression, and anxiety have all been linked to the escalating nationwide high school dropout rate (Greene & Winters, 2006; Greenberg et al. 2001). Therefore, preventing reading failure has become a concern of psychologists and mental health practitioners as they strive to stem behavioral and social problems in school-based settings (Prilleltensky et al., 2001). Failure in the classroom leads to poor psychological adjustment, deficits in mental health development, and dysfunctional behavior (Weissberg, Kumpfer, & Seligman, 2003).

Reading Failure Leads to a Lifetime of Failure

If reading is the catalyst that starts children on the road to failure, then correcting reading deficits early should help prevent later school-based mental health problems (Greenberg et al., 2003). G. Reid Lyon, from the National Institute of Child Health and Child Development, told Congress that correcting reading failure is essential, and that if we correct reading failure in the first grade, then 90 to 95 percent of children improve and learn to read at grade level. He went on to explain that 75 percent of children who read below grade level at the end of third grade never overcome their reading problems (Lyon, 1988).

The inability to read cannot be separated from perceived failure; they must be treated at the same time in order to be truly successfully corrected (Bandura et al., 2001). Therefore, a purely educational skill-building reading program is not enough to alleviate reading failure. Self-efficacy must be rebuilt.

The National Reading Panel (2000) found that small groups were more effective than one-on-one tutoring or classroom instruction as a means of teaching children to read. Groups have also been identified as a highly effective means of counseling with children (Shechtman & Rybko, 2004); therefore, the group setting becomes a natural choice for school-based interventions. But we must be careful, because reading groups stigmatize children.

Codes, colors, and numbers have not proven to be the least bit successful in keeping children from labeling their peers as smart or slow readers. Such a label can have devastating effects on a child's development and adjustment throughout life (Miller & Shinn, 2005; Nelson, Prilleltensky, & Peters, 2003; Ryan & Deci, 2000). Perceived inferiority reduces a child's motivation and ability to learn. If a child thinks he is going to fail, he typically does.

We cannot simply place children in a group and think that the group setting will correct reading failure. Reading groups have been used for years and have not solved the problem (National Reading Panel, 2000). A successful prevention program needs to teach children to read effectively and also to erase the stigmatizing effects of failure.

Because reading is so closely intertwined with our self-identity and early development, the methods that we use in teaching children to read become an integral component of school-based mental health. What happens in the classroom has a direct effect on the child's psychological well-being today and throughout life. Reading is a developmental growth step that the child needs in order to be successful. If the child is not successful in learning to read, the stigmatization of failure marks the child for life.

By reversing the cycle of perceived failure that begins in first grade when children fail, it is possible to make a difference in the child's ability to advance in school, succeed in life, and also prevent later psychological adjustment problems. As Albert Bandura (1995) has shown, negative self-efficacy can be reversed and children can overcome dysfunctional experiences. This is why group-centered interventions work better than traditional counseling or psychoeducational groups in correcting classroom-based problems.

The Group-Centered Approach

Camp Sharigan is an example of a group-centered intervention designed for at-risk readers in the first through third grade (Clanton Harpine, 2007b). It's an interactive ten-hour group intervention that teaches the basic skills that children need if they are to succeed in reading, and that uses group process to alleviate a perceived sense of failure and help children develop a more positive approach to reading. At the same time, it also intrinsically teaches social skills, teamwork, and persistence in completing a task.

In preliminary testing of the Camp Sharigan program, inner-city Hispanic children participating in the program in Texas improved and continued to show improvement one year later (Clanton Harpine & Reid, submitted 2008a), and children who had been labeled at-risk of failing in a suburban Ohio school surpassed the comprehension scores of non at-risk students after only a six-week program (Clanton Harpine, 2005).

Camp Sharigan

Each session at Camp Sharigan begins with an action story that teaches listening skills. On day 1, the story introduces Sharigan, the friendly camp mascot, who teaches the children how to work together to capture tricky words. Then the children receive treasure hunt maps that direct them around the room to each of ten learning centers. As the children travel from one learning center to another, they work in small groups to "capture tricky words" and place each captured word on the paper poison-ivy vine surrounding the room. Instead of saying that a child misspelled or mispronounced a word, at Camp Sharigan the word is *captured*. Labeling words as *tricky* encourages children to work on difficult concepts that they missed in the classroom. Adding an element of play encourages children to work with words. A constructive, group-centered atmosphere turns a simple reversal in terminology (from *missed* to *captured*) into a therapeutic tool that helps children overcome failure.

There are also stories to read or write, spelling words, phonics games, and puppet plays. At one station, children work together in groups to read and follow directions to build a small pop-up house. Camp Guides at each learning center provide one-on-one tutoring as the children travel around the room. Camp Sharigan uses group process to help children overcome their sense of failure and distills a genuine desire to read through use of intrinsic motivation, not prizes or awards.

Each day is different, packed with fun-filled, hands-on learning activities designed to meet the participants' needs. More than just a reading program or educational teaching tool, Camp Sharigan is a group-centered intervention that helps children change from failure to success and stresses self-efficacy, intrinsic motivation, and cohesive group process.

Real-World Applications

Observational Extensions

Observe children in reading groups, one-on-one tutoring, and any other method that your school uses to help children who struggle to read. List the advantages and disadvantages that you see for each method.

A Ready-to-Use Group-Centered Intervention: The Fox's Game

This group-centered intervention is a continuation of the group-centered intervention used in Chapter 2. Unlike the story used in Chapter 5, this is primarily a fun story. Designing and playing a game together works to rebuild self-efficacy and is an excellent group builder.

This intervention was tested in a research study conducted in 2005 with at-risk readers. The at-risk readers outscored those not participating in the intervention on a comprehension quiz (Clanton Harpine, 2005).

Objective: To increase comprehension skills through hands-on activities.
Time Needed: 1 hour

1. Read the following story to the children.
2. Have the children complete the story by writing their own ending.
3. Have the children create a game, making a game board showing where Mr. Bear and his friends and Fox and the geese should stand for the game.
4. Have the children share their stories and games and possibly even play the games as a group.

The Story: "The Adventure" (Part 2)

Mr. Bear and Sister Bear crawled up onto the bank of the island, easing out of the water as quietly as possible. Tuffy crawled up beside Sister Bear and lay sunning in the grass. Blue Jay flew off to scout out the area while the bears rested. Little Sister was very tired, but she didn't want to complain because she was afraid that Mr. Bear would send her back home.

Mr. Bear checked his compass to make sure that they were still headed south. Mr. Bear knew that he lived north of the lake. He assumed that if he kept going south that he would cross the lake and then be able to swim back home. Little sister closed her eyes and dozed. Tuffy was tired too, just from holding on.

Suddenly, Blue Jay came flying in low squawking, "Go, go, quickly into the water, the fox is coming. Quick, we have to get away."

Little Sister Bear was too tired. She couldn't budge.

"We'll talk with this fox," said Mr. Bear. "We'll explain that we mean him no harm and only wish to rest a bit."

"The fox is very tricky. It is better to escape," said Blue Jay.

"We will rest," said Mr. Bear looking at his tired little sister.

"Fox! Fox!" squawked Blue Jay as the cunning old fox approached.

"Good day, kind sir. It is very gracious of you to let us weary travelers stop and rest a bit on the banks of your grand and glorious island. We appreciate your hospitality."

"Yes, yes, you must stay for dinner, for the turtle and the little bear look completely tuckered out," chuckled the cunning Old Fox.

"No, we mustn't stay," squawked Blue Jay. "But it's very kind of you to offer."

"I insist," said the Old Fox. "The geese and I were just about to play a game before dinner. You must join us. We need exactly four more players."

"We haven't time to play any of your games," said Blue Jay. "And besides, you cheat. No one wants to play with you."

"But it would be rude to refuse my hospitality," said the sly Old Fox. "You may even pick berries from my berry patch to refresh you for your journey."

Mr. Bear thought about Sister Bear. She was tired and probably hungry. "We accept your invitation," said Mr. Bear.

"That's a mistake! That's a mistake!" squawked Blue Jay.

Discussion with the Children

"You're the authors. What happens next? What kind of game will they play? Who will win? Will the fox cheat? What will Mr. Bear do? What will the fox do?

Will Mr. Bear be able to outwit the fox? How? What happens next?

7
Designing Group-Centered Motivational Interventions

She stood smiling at me, with the most adorable look on her face, as the camp guide explained, "I can't get her to read, not even one word. She just stands there smiling." "Let's play a game," I said. "Would you like to play a game?" She nodded her head vigorously. "I'll read first, then you." She nodded agreement. I read the first three words on the grapevine. She repeated all three words. I read five words. She repeated all five words. I read ten words. Again, she repeated all ten words. I used a scrap of paper to cover the words as I read them. She repeated every word. I pointed to the next word on the list and said, "Your turn." She wrinkled her nose and giggled. She wasn't reading. She could remember up to ten words at a time and recite them to me perfectly, but she couldn't read. I remembered the teacher telling me that the girl had hearing problems, spoke English as a second language, was lazy, and simply refused to try in class. I didn't think the problem was hearing; she repeated every single word exactly as I had pronounced it, even the list of ten. "Let's play another game." I offered my hand; she grasped it excitedly as I directed her over to Camp Sharigan's Snake Pit. I picked up the alphabet cards. "We want to see how many cards we can each capture." She nodded affirmatively. I started. She held up the cards; I read all six letters and captured all six cards. Next, I read three cards correctly and intentionally missed the last three cards. She still gave me all six cards for being correct. When it was her turn, she would not or could not read the cards. The child had been labeled as lazy and as having a hearing problem when she was actually very bright. She simply could not read, not even the alphabet. She had fallen through the cracks of the system and had been labeled a failure because no one had found the correct way to teach her to read.

Many factors can hinder children's education and development, including family and home environment, poverty, neighborhood influences, discrimination, and the uneven quality of schooling (Black & Krishnakumar, 1998). When children find themselves classified as failures, or consider themselves to be unsuccessful, they become vulnerable to developmental problems and mental disorders (Nelson et al., 2003.) A growing body of evidence shows that prevention programs can enhance a child's ability to learn and promote mental health and wellness (Brooks-Gunn, 2003; Greenberg et al., 2001; Nelson et al., 2003; Prilleltensky et al., 2001).

E. Clanton Harpine, *Group Interventions in Schools.*
© Springer Science + Business Media, LLC 2008

Schools that stress group prevention programs have higher academic achievement, a lower dropout rate, reduced absenteeism and truancy, and fewer behavior problems, such as rejection, teasing, bullying, and fighting (Adelman & Taylor, 2006; Buhs et al., 2006). Group interventions are the most frequently used technique in school-based mental health preventive programs (Noam & Hermann, 2002). Group interventions enhance a child's ability to learn and improve overall mental wellness, which is important in school-based settings (Sandler et al., 2005).

Prevention-focused counseling programs create a climate of healthy well-being and an atmosphere conducive to change (Weissberg, Kumpfer, & Seligman, 2003). Group interventions are the best prevention-oriented counseling approach for school-based settings (Slavin, 2002).

Many school-based mental health prevention programs use either a curriculum-based or a psychoeducational format. While psychoeducational programs have proven effective with certain age groups and for particular problems (Kulic et al., 2004), curriculum-based formats rarely succeed in efficacy-retraining (Pressley, Mohan, Raphael, & Fingeret, 2007). A curriculum-based program also does not take advantage of the therapeutic powers of group cohesion or stress intrinsic motivation. As we stated earlier, each of these three principles are essential for an effective prevention program for academic failure; therefore, if we are to develop effective programs to reduce academic failure, we must design group interventions that incorporate self-efficacy, intrinsic motivation, and cohesive group process.

At present, school-based group programs do not always fully implement the therapeutic power of group process. As discussed in Chapter 5, many counseling programs do not emphasize group process or group cohesion. Yet, group therapy has been shown to be as effective as or even more effective than individual therapy in such situations (Hoag & Burlingame, 1997; Shechtman & Katz, 2007).

Therefore, we need to select or design group interventions that take full advantage of cohesive group process (Piper, Ogrodniczuk, Lamarche, Hilscher, & Joyce, 2005). Merely sitting in a circle or meeting as a group does not fulfill this requirement. We must design group interventions with group cohesion and group process as key essential components of the intervention (Johnson, Pulsipher, Ferrin, Burlingame, Davies, & Gleave, 2006). For group cohesion to develop and grow within a group, the group atmosphere must be positive and intrinsically motivating (Ogrodniczuk & Piper, 2003). Cohesion requires interaction (Holtz, 2004). Group interventions that use groups only as a means of collective instruction do not engage in interaction or achieve cohesion.

Designing Group-Centered Interventions that Encourage Group Cohesion

Group interventions should provide a group in which participants can explore and work together as equal participants in a supportive atmosphere (Marmarosh & Markin, 2007). The group creates an environment. The group environment becomes the agent of change. Cohesion is essential if change is to occur (Marmarosh et al., 2005).

The next question is how do we develop such a group. The group is our agent of change, and it is how we design our group experience that determines whether that experience will be successful or unsuccessful. Group-centered interventions create a safe intrinsic group setting where group members can practice school-based, classroom-oriented interpersonal skills. Our next objective, then, is to outline a step-by-step plan for developing effective group-centered interventions for children and teenagers:

Step 1: Define the problem or assess the needs of the group with which you wish to work.
Step 2: Design a program using the full power of group process is to create an atmosphere that encourages group cohesion.
Step 3: Combine self-efficacy, intrinsic motivation, and cohesive group process into one prevention program.

We turn first to the needs of the participants. Remember that our school-based prevention program may be held before school, during school, after school, or through community-based organizations. The key ingredient is that we are working to erase academic failure.

Step 1: Developing Group Interventions to Meet the Needs of Students

First, define the problem. This may be through a needs assessment of the client population or through informal interviews or observations from a focus group.

Try to determine the advantages and disadvantages of the existing program or approach to handling the problem. Is there a need for a change or a new program? If there is a need, what has caused this need?

You cannot develop an effective group intervention unless you design your new program to address the needs of the participants. Too often we design programs to address the needs of schools instead of those of students. If your group intervention program is trying to help a particular group of students in a school-based setting, then it must meet those students' needs.

Assessing needs is a crucial step. Let us consider our example of academic failure from the opening case study. If a child is in third grade but cannot read at grade level, who has failed? Is it the child, the school, or both? If we design a program to meet the needs of the classroom teacher, will that necessarily meet the needs of the child? If our program is to help the child learn to read, then we must ask why the child has failed to learn to read. The child's needs become the group intervention program's central focus. A successful group intervention must answer the needs of the failing child rather than the needs of the school or the teacher. Sometimes needs are combined, but the child's needs must prevail; otherwise, your program will fail.

We must also remember that each participant brings unique individual needs to the group. These needs may be similar to other group members' needs, or they may be totally different. An effective group-centered intervention must meet the needs of all group participants. When designing a new group intervention, we must look at the group as both a collection of unique individuals and a group of individuals who will interact and work together. The means through which we shape group interaction will often determine our group intervention's success or failure.

Cohesion is essential. We build cohesion in a group by adapting group process to the needs of the participants. Structure and rules are necessary requirements of a successful group, but group members must identify with and adopt these rules and structure. Therefore, our first step in designing a group-centered intervention is to identify the needs of those who will participate in the group.

A Worksheet for Assessing the Needs of the Group

Description of Group:

Description of individual clients in the group (focus on interaction, personality, self-concept, and self-efficacy):

What problem would you like the group to work on or change? (If there is a diagnostic code, please identify.)

Why have you grouped these students together in a group? How can they help each other?

Is cohesion high or low in your group right now?

How can you make the group more cohesive?

Why is there a need for a change? How will the change benefit the group?

What are your goals for the group? What do you hope to achieve with the group?

What are the goals of the group members? What would they like to achieve?

Are there any group problems that you haven't identified? Do you plan to work on these problems? Why or why not?

A Needs Assessment Checklist

Performing a needs assessment should provide an overview of the group with which you will be working. This will help you determine the most effective structure for your group intervention. Before going on, review the checklist below and make sure that you have fully analyzed the needs of your group:

1. Determine whether there is a need for a change or a new program.
2. What has caused that need?
3. What are the needs of the students who will participate in your program?
4. If you are proposing a change or a new group intervention program, how will your program meet the needs of the participants? How will your new group intervention program bring about the desired change?
5. What are the advantages of having this group meet together? What are the disadvantages? What problems will you encounter in implementing your group intervention?

Step 2: How Would You Design a Program Using the Full Power of Group Process?

Cohesion does not simply happen when children or teens are placed in a group. Cohesion must be built into the group prevention program. You must create an atmosphere that encourages group cohesion. You must create a group experience that allows interaction.

Working with Children

When working with children, I always incorporate an element of play in my group-centered interventions. Play stimulates and encourages children to interact and get involved with others in a group. Since I want to encourage interaction in order to build a cohesive group, I also include hands-on activities.

Play does not have to be open-ended; it can be directed. Children need structure, but the structure must not stifle cohesion.

An example comes from a bright third-grade girl whose parents signed her up to participate in my Camp Sharigan program because she had received a low score on her standardized reading comprehension test at school. When she arrived, she hid in the hallway and refused to join the group. To her, the program was for those who had failed the test. After a few minutes of listening to the laughter and delight of the children as they moved around the room from learning center to learning center, she emerged and participated in the group to the point of begging her mother to let her stay longer when the mother arrived to pick her up.

Camp Sharigan teaches spelling words, phonics, story writing, and oral reading. The exact same skills taught in the classroom, but Camp Sharigan teaches these skills in a hands-on play group structure.

Play is a part of a child's natural developmental learning process. Children express their feelings and problems more comfortably through play. Playing together creates a nurturing environment where children feel accepted and safe and are thereby willing to risk exploring learning tasks that may be difficult for them or at which they may have failed in a traditional classroom.

Many of my programs are held after school. Children are hungry, tired, and often upset from their day at school. For example, a sweet, normally smiling girl arrived directly from school one day with a frown on her face. She stomped her foot, refused to participate, and was unhappy about something that had taken place at school that day. I started her at the learning center station that was working on constructing a paper pop-up book. She was compliant but unhappy. In a matter of minutes, her frown was replaced by enthusiasm, and eventually a smile, as she worked hard to make furniture to go in her pop-up storybook. Her enthusiasm continued throughout the entire two-hour session as she traveled around the room to all ten learning centers.

The ultimate goal of a group-centered intervention is to enable children to resume normal development and to boost their ability to thrive in the future; therefore, a group-centered intervention designed to erase academic failure should address the cause of academic failure while teaching the skills that children need to erase such failure. In school-based settings, helping children develop new pathways for learning material that they were unsuccessful in learning in the classroom helps to meet this goal. The hands-on play activities that I use in my group-centered Camp Sharigan intervention are built around the reading, spelling, phonics, and comprehension problems that arose in the classroom.

Play provides a motivational environment where children can learn basic skills and allows children to work at mastery of a task at their own pace. Play serves as a medium for practicing social skills, teamwork, and group participation. Learning and change occur through play by structuring the child's behaviors. Structuring can include anything from selecting activities to setting limits on acceptable and unacceptable behavior. Challenging hands-on play activities encourage children to learn.

Puppets can help to teach phonics. Craft projects and step-by-step directions can increase comprehension skills. A pop-up storybook project can encourage a reluctant child to read, and even to write a story.

Play creates an atmosphere that is conducive to learning. Hands-on play activities motivate children to tackle hard tasks from the classroom that they have either given up on learning or failed to accomplish, but a group-centered intervention is more than just a fun way to learn. It is also a curative experience. The environment that you create motivates children not only to want to learn but also to enjoy learning. By improving the child's ability to learn, we enhance the child's perceived acceptance by fellow classmates. Perceived acceptance motivates the child to see learning in a positive light and thereby be more willing to meet the daily challenges of the classroom.

Early intervention through school or community-based prevention programs can prevent academic failure and retention. Portable group therapy programs such as Camp Sharigan can greatly increase the number of children receiving therapeutic help. Preventing failure within a child's early stages of development heightens the individual's chances for a happy, well-adjusted productive life.

Children do not learn the same way as adults do. Children learn by doing, through their actions, experiences, and by experimenting. As you develop group interventions for children, build in an element of play that encourages exploration. Instead of working from the usual spelling list where the teacher counts how many words the student has wrong, at Camp Sharigan a word that a child cannot pronounce, read, or spell becomes not a word "missed" but a new "tricky word to capture and learn." Learning words becomes a game rather than a grade.

The mood that a child brings to a group intervention program may affect that child's willingness to cooperate, learn, and change. Mood is one of the variables in motivation that determines an individual's willingness to perform a particular action or engage in learning (Grawitch, David, Munz, & Kramer, 2003).

Hands-on play activities intrinsically motivate children to interact and participate. Play sets an atmosphere that enables the child to learn and develop a positive self-concept, pride, and a feeling of accomplishment. Combining hands-on play activities with intrinsic motivation encourages a child to become more self-directed.

When developing effective group-centered interventions for children, I feel that hands-on play activities are essential. They fit into Bandura's (1995) four requirements for rebuilding self-efficacy as discussed in Chapter 2. Hands-on play activities are naturally intrinsic and do not need awards or prizes to motivate children to work on difficult school tasks (Clanton Harpine, 2005). Play encourages interaction and teamwork while building positive group cohesion as children learn to work together and help each other. An atmosphere of play can be both instructive and curative. Therefore, I recommend using hands-on play activities set in an atmosphere of play for your group-centered intervention.

A Worksheet for Developing Group Process

What is the academic problem that you wish to correct?

Do all members of your group have the same degree of difficulty with this problem? How will you adjust for the difference in skill levels and abilities? Describe each participant's needs and how you will adapt to these needs with your intervention.

What activities will you use to rebuild self-efficacy? How will they meet Bandura's (1995) four requirements, as listed in Chapter 2?

How are your group activities intrinsic rather than extrinsic? Are you using any extrinsic motivators? Why?

How will you use group process to bring about change with your group?

What activities will you use to encourage cohesion? Will these activities also help rebuild self-efficacy? How?

Does your group-centered intervention meet the needs of your participants as described in your needs assessment?

Working with Teenagers

The same worksheet can be used in developing group-centered interventions for teenagers. With teens, I incorporate community service, drama, clowning, or some other action-oriented activity. Yes, they are teenagers, but they still learn best through their actions. Problem solving is best taught by organizing and planning a group activity. Cooperation and respect for fellow classmates is often taught most effectively through service to others. Working on a project together builds cohesion within a group. Correcting remedial academic failure can often be taught most effectively by helping those who struggle more than you.

The group of teenagers described in Chapter 2 is a perfect example. They blamed all their problems on someone else. They spent all of their time creating scapegoats for their failure in the classroom and for their failure in making friends with others at school. It was always someone else's fault. Creating a drama group and writing their own play allowed the group to work on academic skills: reading, writing, sentence structure, and spelling. The hands-on nature of the drama group also encouraged them to think about their behavior and how their behavior was perceived by others.

As they wrote, they began to reflect. Why would a person think this way? Why would a person feel this way? Why would a person speak this way to someone else? What kind of response are you seeking when you speak in such a manner?

By writing their own play, the group members were able to express their feelings and fears in a way that they would not have been able to express in a traditional counseling group. They had been in counseling before; they had refused to consider any point of view but their own. Hands-on group-centered activities rebuild self-efficacy and use the intrinsic curative power of cohesive group process to change behavior.

Group process is only effective in changing behavior if you fully utilize group interaction and strive to build a cohesive group. An instructional group or a curriculum-based group is not cohesive, and therefore does not bring about a change in behavior. Teenagers, as much if not more than children, need hands-on activities in a cohesive group. Group process does not happen automatically when you gather teens together. Group process must be designed into your group intervention.

A Group Process Checklist

1. Describe your group-centered intervention.
2. What is unique about your program?
3. How will you bring about the desired change or meet the needs listed in your needs assessment?
4. How will your program meet the needs of all participants?
5. What are the advantages of your program?
6. What are the disadvantages of your program?
7. How will you create a cohesive group atmosphere?
8. How will you encourage group interaction?

9. What will you do to help group members get involved with the group?
10. Write a clear, concise program proposal. Make sure to incorporate the principles of self-efficacy, intrinsic motivation, and group cohesion into your group-centered intervention prevention program.

Step 3: Combining Self-Efficacy, Intrinsic Motivation, and Cohesive Group Process into One Prevention Program

When we combine self-efficacy, intrinsic motivation, and cohesive group process together we build a group-centered intervention that can help both children and teens erase failure and change unwanted behavior. If we delete any of these essential three requirements, we destroy the power that the group has to bring about change. In other words, we cannot insert prizes or awards in place of hands-on intrinsic motivators, because extrinsic rewards will destroy the internal, intrinsic desire necessary to rebuild self-efficacy. In the same way, we cannot merely gather a group together to make it more convenient to talk with or lecture to a group on how they should change their behavior. If you want to design a successful group-centered intervention, you must incorporate self-efficacy, intrinsic motivation, and cohesive group process.

Developing a Group for Children

In Chapter 6, I described the Camp Sharigan program for children as an example of a group-centered intervention. Programs such as Camp Sharigan teach reading, erase failure, and restore self-efficacy.

Most after-school programs function as extensions of the traditional school day. Worksheets, reading groups, and tutoring fail to solve the real problem. Worksheets do not teach, nor do stickers; therefore, programs based on extrinsic rewards are doomed to failure. An effective prevention program helps the individual change (Weinstein, 2006).

After-school programs that incorporate self-efficacy, intrinsic motivational skill building, and group cohesion can be set up within our present public school system. Many schools offer an after-school program for at-risk readers, but utilize the same teaching strategies under which the child failed to learn to read in the classroom. What is needed is an after-school prevention program that takes a totally different approach to learning. When such an approach is used, as with Camp Sharigan, then the child has the opportunity to relearn without the stigma of previous failure.

Developing a Group for Teenagers

Group-centered interventions can also help teenagers. I am designing and testing a group-centered intervention for reducing health risk behaviors in teens. The teenage group is a service-oriented group, but the theoretical base is still the same. The group must emphasize self-efficacy, use intrinsic motivation, and stress cohesive group process.

After-school prevention programming can be an effective way to provide mental health services to large numbers of teenagers. Longitudinal research shows that early intervention through school-based prevention programs can reduce violence, underage drinking, teen pregnancy, disruptive behavior, and low achievement (Hawkins, Castalano, Kosterman, Abbott, & Hill, 1999). School-based prevention programs may also provide a positive alternative to students who otherwise face being retained.

Developing decision-making skills can be one of the best opportunities for young people to experiment in a safe group environment with limits and control. A healthy, cohesive group also needs the safety to foster an authentic sharing of feelings and ideas. Teenagers need to feel they have a sense of control and influence over the workings and actions of their group. Also, they need to be able to express their true feelings without reservations or worry about the consequences of self-disclosure. They also need to learn to compromise within the group. The more group members interact together and share their ideas, the more likely the group will be to develop and accomplish its goals. Groups with high interaction and cohesion tend to be more productive. Cohesion is the result of a positive climate, free involvement, and open and safe interaction between all members.

In organizing a new group, development must include group climate, involvement, interaction, cohesion, and productivity. Climate is the emotional structure of the group. Involvement is more than just attendance; it is how committed members are to the group. Interaction between all group members must be free and open. Cohesion is the glue that holds the group together. Productivity focuses on the accomplishments of the group and the satisfaction members feel with those accomplishments. Satisfaction leads to positive interaction, and strong group cohesion leads to productive change.

If you are designing a new group intervention program, I offer a checklist of twenty-five rules for program design to help you ensure that your new program is meeting the needs of the participants for whom you are designing the group intervention.

Twenty-Five Rules or Questions to Address in Program Design: A Checklist for Writing a Program Proposal

1. State why there is a need for a change.
2. State what needs to be changed.
3. Explain how your proposal will fulfill or correct this need.
4. Explain why your proposal would be better at meeting this need than other proposals presently available or in use.
5. Explain why your proposal will combat or alleviate the causes of the problem or need.

6. Allow for and take into consideration the individual needs, interests, and concerns of the people who will be participating in your program.

7. Identify the physiological, psychological, and social needs of the participants in your program, and indicate how your proposal meets these needs.

8. Take into account the divergent personalities and the self-concepts of all participants, and allow for diversity.

9. Explain the role of communication in your program, how participants communicate with one another, and whether the group is large, small, or uses teams. Does it use written or computer communication? Is cognitive processing a factor in your program? Are handicaps accommodated? What adjustments will you make? What will you do to encourage interaction in the group?

10. Are there language barriers or cultural differences? How will you adjust for the diversity of your group members? What will you do to make sure that each group member feels included as a full participant?

11. Will there be a means for expression of grievances or complaints? To whom will participants complain and how?

12. How will individuals measure compliance, improvement, or change with your program? Will participants be able to notice change on a daily, weekly, monthly, or yearly basis?

13. Does your program use extrinsic or intrinsic motivators? How will your program incorporate intrinsic motives?

14. Do you avoid using rewards, punishment, or extrinsic incentives?

15. If you must use extrinsic motivators, what are the hidden psychological costs? Are the costs justified? Would it be possible to conduct your program without using extrinsic motivators or rewards?

16. What are your goals for the project? Will the program that you have designed meet these goals?

17. What are the advantages of your program?

18. What are the disadvantages?

19. Can you reduce or eliminate the disadvantages? If you cannot eliminate a disadvantage, can you minimize its effect on participants?

20. What will you do if participants to not comply or show positive results from your program? How will you adapt?

21. What is the financial cost of your program? Who will pay? Can the cost be reduced? How do you justify the financial cost to participants or supporting organization?

22. How much time must participants devote to your program? Will participants be expected to devote time away from the program as well, such as with practice or specialized training? Where will the program be held? Will transportation be a problem?

23. Describe your program clearly in a formal written proposal or verbally. Can others understand exactly what you propose to do and why?

24. Is the unique nature of your program clear? Can others immediately ascertain how your program would be different? Explain why this uniqueness is good.

25. Does anything about your program proposal trouble you? Can you fix the problem or must you work around the problem? If you can fix the problem, how will you do so? If you must work around the problem, how will you do so when conducting the program?

Real-World Applications

Observational Extensions

Observe children in a kindergarten. Do they seem more motivated than children in first grade? Why? Is intrinsic or extrinsic motivation being used?

Observe children in first through fourth grades. How is motivation different in each grade?

If possible, observe a middle school and a high school; do you see intrinsic or extrinsic motivators being used? Why?

A Ready-to-Use Group-Centered Intervention: The Paper Plate Puppet Play

This group-centered intervention works with both children and teens alike. Working together as a cooperative group always provides an excellent opportunity for cohesion.

Puppets can help children explore problems that they have experienced in the classroom. Even teenagers enjoy making puppets. Puppets can help teenagers discuss problems that they are reluctant to discuss in a group setting.

Writing a puppet play allows children to analyze the play more completely. A written puppet play allows them to reanalyze their thoughts later to explore patterns of growth and change.

Puppets are excellent intrinsic motivators and can help children rebuild self-efficacy in reading and writing. Working together as a group builds cohesion.

Objective: To reinforce writing as a means of exploring problems in the classroom.
Time: One session for making puppets and one session for writing puppet play
Supplies needed: Supplies can be simple or elaborate:
Paper plate
Construction paper
Popsicle stick, ruler, or yardstick
Scissors
Glue
Stapler and tape
Felt, cloth, or paper bags
Fake fur or yarn
Decorations

Glitter for rainbow
Coffee and plastic (Easter) grass for tree
Aluminum foil or wrapping paper
Polyester stuffing
Chenille stems
Yellow streamer
Tempera paint and brushes, markers, crayons

Paper plates provide a simple and inexpensive way to make puppets and even simple scenery for a puppet play. You can make very simple puppets or more elaborate puppets.

Puppets can be made with all sorts of materials: long paper curls, springy legs, tall hats, braided yarn hair, fake fur beards, painted faces, glitter, sequins, and even buttons for eyes. Use tan and brown paper plates for skin color. Plain white plates can also be painted, colored with crayons, or covered with paper to give the color you want for the puppet's skin. You can also make animal puppets or make-believe characters of any color. When you cut slashes in paper for eyelashes, bangs, grass, and flowers as described, cut down to about one-quarter-inch of the edge. Stop before you cut all the way across so that your slashes do not fall apart. You need that uncut edge to glue the eyelash in place.

To make a little girl with glasses and long paper curls or a little boy with glasses, proceed as follows:

1. Draw eyes and mouth on paper. Cut out. Shape a scrap of skin colored paper into a triangle for the nose. Glue each into place on a skin colored paper plate.
2. Cut tiny slashes into one-inch squares of paper for eyelashes. Curl the fringed edge of each eyelash on a pencil and glue in place above eye.
3. Trace around a glass that fits over eyes. (Foil paper makes shiny glasses.) Place a penny next to your first circle to connect circles. Trace second circle and over penny.
4. Draw smaller inside circles or use a smaller glass. Trace penny to complete bridge on glasses. Add side pieces to make glasses fit face. Glue into place only on outside edge.
5. Cut six strips of eleven-inch-long paper for hair. Roll ends onto a pencil for curl. Glue curls to edge of plate above glasses. Glue or tape ruler or stick onto back of plate for handle.
6. Trace top of plate on paper for bangs. The bangs should cover top of curls but not cover glasses. Cut small slashes for bangs. Glue into place.
7. To make a boy puppet, trace top of plate and cut short hair.

Children can also make scenery for their puppet play. A tree, a beautiful rainbow, flowers, a rain cloud, and a smiling sun can all be made from paper plates to provide scenery for a puppet play:

1. Staple six small paper plates together in a circular pattern to make tree. Cut trunk from stiff large plates. Tape the tree to a yard stick. Paint or cover with paper.

2. Cut a cloud shape from a large paper plate. Cut raindrops, cover with foil, and hang with string from back of cloud. Glue stuffing on. To hide handle, cover with black paper.
3. Draw and color flowers on a plate. Cut around edges. For puffy flower, cut slashes in paper. Glue layers one on top of the other for puffy effect. Add handle.
4. Cut a paper plate in half. Tear scrap paper into little squares. Glue into a rainbow pattern. Place on a black covered stick for handle.
5. Make a friendly sun with a smiley face. Cut slashes on a yellow paper streamer if you want rays for your sun.

8
Creating Cohesive Group Interventions

My first introduction to the teenager was when she attended a one-day after-school reading program that I was conducting in a neighboring town. She seemed excited to learn and eager to read. She was a bit shy, but worked hard during the four-hour program.

Her discipline record from school was filled with a long string of problems. She had been banned from the school bus and placed in a classroom for learning-disabled students. She tested at the pre-primer level in reading for first grade. She was thirteen years old. Her file said, "Will probably drop out soon."

The next time we met was at a Saturday program for at-risk students. She did not fit the description spelled out in her discipline record from school, but she was also not the hard-working, eager-to-learn girl of my first encounter. This time, she was with a group of her peers.

Three different group settings created three different group behaviors.

Groups are comprised of individuals. Every individual is different, has a different personality, attitudes, values, experiences, and way of dealing with people. No two people perceive or react to life in exactly the same way. Even identical twins react to the world differently (Segal, 1999). Situational influences are constantly changing. The individual person lies at the center of this constant flow of influence.

Individuals structure and interpret the world in which they live through their perceptions. Regardless of whether these perceptions are correct or incorrect, they become the perceived reality of the individual (Rogers, 1951).

When we join a group, we bring our entire field of experience with us. We bring our perceptions, misperceptions, attitudes, fears, values, social experiences, and feelings. It is by evaluating our feelings that we make decisions (Damasio, 1994). Therefore, to understand individual differences, we must understand the individual's self-image or perceived view of self. From our perception of self we form our projected image. It is this projected image that we bring with us when we join a new group; who we want to be or who we want others to think we are is called our projected image.

The girl in our opening example changed her projected image to fit the expectations of each group. We often encounter these expectations when we organize school-based group interventions. Children who fail in the classroom often retain

E. Clanton Harpine, *Group Interventions in Schools.*
© Springer Science + Business Media, LLC 2008

that image in a counseling group. Teenagers who gain group status with peers through disruptive behavior feel an obligation to maintain such behavior when they are in a group of their peers.

If you have the opportunity to select the membership for a group intervention, then, as illustrated in the opening example, placing disruptive students in a group from outside their sphere of friends can be constructive. In school-based situations, disruptive students are often pulled out of class and sent to groups because of their behavior. In that case, you must build a group structure that will enable them to change as a group.

Merely discussing misbehavior as a group usually leads to more examples of misbehavior. If you change the focus of the group to a hands-on activity, then you have an opportunity to change the members' self-image and group behavior because you reconstruct how participants act in a group setting.

An example comes from a group of third-grade girls. This was a fairly typical group of children, except that they had difficulty getting along with one another. They bickered and argued constantly, finding fault with one another. They were also stingy and refused to share. As Christmas approached, I gave each girl a stuffed teddy bear to sew and dress for a needy child for Christmas. The girls spent weeks working on the bears. As they worked, they had to share the same piece of cloth and remember to measure the lace correctly so that there would be enough for everyone. Some bears had bonnets and frilly dresses; others were dressed in overalls. Each girl had placed a bit of her own personality into her project. The girls received recognition in the local newspaper, and were very proud of their accomplishment. I noticed that, as a group, they argued less and began to accept one another more. Their classroom teacher remarked how the girls had even chosen to work together on a group project in the classroom. They also signed up to do another community service project. A hands-on community service project that required the group to share supplies and materials erased classroom competition. Petty arguments were replaced by cooperation that transferred back to the classroom setting.

The Advantage of Hands-On Interaction

In a traditional counseling group, the intermingling of personalities and projection of self-images consumes the initial phase of a new group. The focus is on inclusion and acceptance, which often leads to anxiety and conflict (Wheelan, 2005). With a group-centered intervention, the focus is on the hands-on task. Shifting the focus of the group from self-image to hands-on activity allows new group behaviors to replace old behavior patterns. If we are to change personality, interpersonal behaviors, or group behavior drawn from peers, we must create a group structure within which students can safely interact and test these new behaviors (Magen & Mangiardi, 2005).

Personality changes through interaction with others (Yalom & Leszcz, 2005). We must change the student's self-image before we can change their projected image and resulting behavior. Improving interpersonal communication in a group setting is the first step.

Effective interpersonal communication can only grow through positive group interaction. Hostility, anger, reprimands, or accusations do not lead to positive interaction. We must instead translate disruptive behavior and classroom failure into constructive acts, and then through constructive acts show new ways of acting in the classroom.

Interaction Leads to Cohesion

Cohesion is the strength of group process. For students to erase failure and change unwanted behaviors, they must undergo a new, positive group experience, one where they rebuild self-efficacy and learn to interact successfully with peers. Children and teens must experience success and change; mere insight, instruction, or new knowledge is not sufficient (Yalom & Leszcz, 2005).

The group intervention must focus on the here-and-now, not the disruptive behavior that happened back in the classroom. It is through constructive group interaction that group members develop a cohesive, positive bond. It is this positive, cohesive bond that helps individuals change their misperceptions and faulty self-images (Ablon & Jones, 2002).

For example, the Camp Sharigan program builds a cohesive, positive bond through the intrinsic atmosphere of play. The play atmosphere of the camp encourages reluctant children to get involved and controls disruptive children through hands-on activities and the learning center structure. Learning centers allow children to work at their own pace. One-on-one tutors at the learning centers provide needed instruction as children move around the room. Play encourages interaction. Older children help younger children. There is no competition. Intrinsic play is fun for everyone. Cooperation and working together builds cohesion. The cohesive group process instilled through the Camp Sharigan activities are the by-product of all the group forces acting together on the children to create a feeling of warmth, comfort, safety, sense of belonging, and a feeling that they are valued, accepted, and allowed to explore new ways of learning (Yalom & Leszcz, 2005). This cohesion is built out of the structure of the group intervention. The combination of efficacy retraining, intrinsic motivation, and cohesive group process make the Camp Sharigan program work successfully to erase academic failure.

This same hands-on approach can be created with teens. For example, select a nursing home or assisted-living facility in your neighborhood that will allow teenagers to visit. Have your group plan a party for the residents, complete with refreshments and games.

Work as a group to plan the party. Encourage the teenagers to bring some of their favorite board games to the nursing home for the party. Seniors enjoy playing board games. Puppets, skits, and songs are also good ideas. Simple crafts even work, and the residents enjoy party hats and streamers.

Working together in a group to plan a party is an excellent group cohesion exercise. Planning a party for lonely seniors is a growth experience for any group. By planning a party for others, the teens must use group interaction and decision-making skills, and they get to experience compassion and caring for others. When we stop thinking about our own wants and needs and begin to think about the needs of others, personal growth begins to occur.

This personal growth is not obtained through mere discussion or group games designed to initiate interaction. Games can be fun and can be constructive ways to initiate interaction, but they do not create a cohesive group. It takes more than just a fun activity to generate group cohesion.

Cohesion is more than just planning happy activities for others. Cohesion is measured by the degree of involvement of all group members, feelings of acceptance, mutual support, lack of conflict in the group, and overall feelings of happiness and well-being (Yalom & Leszcz, 2005).

We create cohesion through the group atmosphere. Hands-on activities allow group members to grow and develop as a group. Acceptance and understanding from a group is one of the most important elements we have to offer another person. Group members often become more accepting of themselves as they become more accepting of others. You cannot accept someone else with their strengths and weaknesses unless you can accept and acknowledge your own strengths and weaknesses (Yalom & Leszcz, 2005).

Membership, acceptance, and approval are very important to children and teenagers, and contribute to their self-image. The successful completion of a group experience can be curative, and can also build a cohesive group base from which to tackle other group problems.

The clown group described in Chapter 4 is an example of a group that used hands-on clowning activities to grow in their understanding of their own self-image. The clowns used the intrinsic kindness of giving to others to heal and change their own behavior. They developed a strong cohesive bond as they helped one another go to hospitals and nursing homes to interact with people who were sick or lonely. As they created and discussed their clown costumes and makeup designs, they also discussed their personalities, their fears, their dreams, and who they wanted to become. Acceptance as a clown and as a member of the clown troupe replaced their fear of rejection by their peers. Change resulted, change that might last a lifetime.

Research shows that community service activities are among the most successful ways to deter risky health behaviors (drugs, alcohol, sex) among teens (Mahoney, 2000). Therefore, group interventions that incorporate community service fit the needs of teens in school-based settings.

Children and teens often have trouble constructively talking about their problems or understanding why they act as they do. Hands-on intrinsic group activities enable young people to apply what they are learning to the group and to school-based situations outside of the group.

Acceptance Is Crucial to Cohesion

One of the best ways to help children and teens gain a perspective on their own problems is through community service. Have your group plan a menu, do the shopping, and, if possible, cook dinner for a needy family. Collecting canned goods is not the same as preparing a meal and delivering it to someone in need.

Hands-on activities are intrinsic, and working together as a group is cohesion building. The planning, compromising, and teamwork required are excellent skill builders. Competition is destructive over time (Deci & Ryan, 1985). Working together to accomplish a common goal is curative. Children and teens need to learn how to work together in groups to solve problems, make decisions, work out compromises, and help and care for one another. Learning to work cooperatively with others is a lifelong skill that can only be learned through practice.

Children and teens find acceptance through being in a group when they participate actively in the group's activities. Hands-on activities encourage all group members to get involved. The task becomes a group project. Everyone cooks; everyone cleans; everyone works together.

Similarly, children work together and help each other to complete the hands-on projects at Camp Sharigan. Children and teens work together to cook a dinner for a needy family or plan a party for a nursing home. Through the act of sharing, helping, and working together as a group, acceptance of self and others begins.

A group creates a living, self-regulating, interactive, protected environment (Luft, 1984). Group membership influences how children and teenagers think. Constructive, positive groups can lead to constructive, positive thinking. It is the structure of the group that makes it either constructive or destructive. Group structure hinges on the atmosphere that you create in the group. An atmosphere of play for children and an atmosphere of service to others for teens creates a structure within the group that allows a cohesive group process to grow. Structure is essential and one of the key ingredients of a successful group. The structure that we use in developing group interventions can lead either to cohesion or to ineffective group process.

A group is composed of individuals. These individuals have different personalities, different wants and needs, different fears, and different self-images. To construct group interventions that lead to cohesion, we must use the full power of cohesive group process, intrinsic motivation, and rebuild self-efficacy. Mere placement in a group is not enough. The group must provide a framework for change.

Sometimes the change is noticed immediately, and sometimes it is gradual. I worked with a group of children and teens through a community-based organization. Every year, we cooked Thanksgiving dinner for a needy family. One year, we learned of a single parent with two small children who had undergone major surgery. The group delivered a hot Thanksgiving dinner to the family on Thanksgiving Day, but that was not the end of the project. The group went on to decorate and deliver a Christmas tree, Christmas presents, and Christmas dinner to the family. Later, the group planned a birthday party, complete with cake, streamers, and games for both children. Several years later, group members still kept in touch with the family. They had learned to care. They had also learned to work together as a group to accomplish a group project. By working together, they have become more cohesive. Through becoming a more cohesive group, they learned to be more accepting of one another and to help one another.

There is no one formula for cohesion. Cohesion is derived through the structure and function of working together as a positive and supportive group. Hands-on activities help children and teens focus on cohesive group process. Intrinsically motivating activities help children and teens rebuild self-efficacy, and to better understand their own individual differences and self-image.

Cohesion grows from within the group. It is derived through acceptance and constructively working toward a common goal. Cohesion is essential in order for group process to be successful. Without cohesion, the curative power of the group is lost.

Real-World Applications

Observational Extensions

Observe friendship groups. Do they include others or do they tend to exclude others from joining their group? Which behaviors invite others to join the group, and which behaviors exclude others?

A Ready-to-Use Group-Centered Intervention: "The Auction"

This is an excellent group-centered intervention for increasing cohesion in a group. The T-shirt portion of the intervention also encourages group members to work together and to think and act kindly toward each other.

Objective: To encourage teenagers to explore their self-image and learn to think of the needs of others.

Time: 1 hour.

Supplies needed: photocopy "Auction" handout, paper T-shirt (simply draw a T-shirt design on paper), a make-believe $5000 check for each group participant, markers, pencils, calculator if desired

Recruit teen volunteers to help with the auction beforehand. You will need (1) an auctioneer, (2) a cashier to list the selling price for each item and the buyer, and (3) a treasurer to keep track of how much money each person has spent. Pick someone to be the auctioneer who can make the auction fun. It will be the treasurer's job to remind people when they are out of money and can no longer bid, so the treasurer keeps a tally of how much money each person spends during the auction.

1. Pass out a $5000 check and auction handout to each group member. Greet members, saying, "I am so pleased to see you that I am going to pay you $5000 just for coming today. Here's your check. We're having an auction in a few minutes, so go over the inventory and decide how you want to spend your money."
2. Keep the auction lively and fast paced.
3. After the auction, have the treasurer report the highest and lowest bid. Discuss the significance of what people were willing to bid on. What does that tell us about ourselves?

4. It is often said that to make lasting friendships, we must think less about what we want and more about whether our friend feels accepted and important in the group. Which items on the auction inventory were directed toward filling the needs of self? Which items were directed toward fulfilling the needs of others? (All of the items listed for auction were directed toward self, except for items 9 and 11 on the auction handout [see below]). Allow time for the group members to talk about the inventory items if they seem interested.
5. Pass out the paper T-shirts. Have your group members divide into pairs, preferably pairing with someone they do not know very well.
6. Ask group members to write their name in the middle of their shirt with fancy letters. Tell them, "You can make animal shapes, buildings, cars, faces, or just abstract drawings. Be creative and have fun."
7. Ask the group members to list what they would look for in a friend. Give suggestions to get everyone started: "I want a friend to be understanding, trustworthy, likable, a good listener, happy, caring, reliable." Partners may help each other.
8. Have the members write a positive characteristic that describes their partner: kind, creative, truthful, reliable, likable, smart, nonjudgmental, trustworthy, fun to be around, helpful. Emphasize that all comments must be positive.

To be true friends, we must accept how others look or act without being judgmental. We must set aside our own need to have people like us, and turn instead to thinking of the fears and problems of others. Have the group plan a group project that will include everyone and strengthen friendship.

Auction Inventory Handout

"You have been given $5000 in pretend money to participate in an auction. Quickly mark in the left column how much you would be willing to pay for each item listed. It may be worth only $1 to you, or it may be worth the entire $5000. You may bid on as many items as you wish. You are not required to bid on items that are not important to you. Once the auction starts, all bids will be made orally. Be ready to shout out how much you would pay for each item as it comes up for sale:"

1. To be the most popular person at school this year, the person everyone admires and looks up to.
2. To have one good friend. Someone who always likes you no matter what you say or do, someone who always wants to be with you or just have you around.
3. To have a beautiful body. To be considered the prettiest or most handsome person in the world.
4. To have beautiful hair.
5. To be the perfect, ideal weight.
6. To be taller.
7. To have beautiful straight teeth without having to wear braces.
8. To be smarter and make straight A's.

9. To be a friend who listens well to what others say. Someone who will sit down and talk with anyone, even if they are unpopular.
10. To be a member of the in-crowd.
11. To never say a negative or harsh word to another person as long as you live.
12. To be able to live up to all of your parents' expectations.
13. To never have to work. Have the freedom to do absolutely nothing if you please.
14. To be in control of those around you. To be able to make others do what you want them to do.
15. To be voted most outstanding player in athletics this year.
16. To have lots of friends.
17. To make everyone think and say nice things about you.
18. To have the ability to make friends instantly with anyone you meet.
19. To have everyone like you regardless of what you do or say.
20. To fall in love and live happily ever after just like in the fairy tales.
21. To be able to escape from all of your problems.
22. To get rid of all stress and pressures around you and be in total control of your own emotions and actions.
23. To be able to change your life and start over.
24. To be a millionaire.
25. To be famous. To achieve something noteworthy and be included in history books of the future.
26. To win every competition you enter, from sports, to music, to getting a date with the most popular person in your group.
27. To be the leader of every group you join.
28. To be totally in charge of your own life and make all your own decisions.
29. To have no one tease or make fun of you for the rest of your life.
30. To always succeed at everything you try to do.

9
Implementing and Evaluating Your Program: The Long-Term Goal

The youth group was essentially dead when I arrived on the scene. The entire com-
munity-based organization was on the verge of extinction. The beloved director had
retired and the new director did not seem to fully understand the needs of the mem-
bers of this long-standing community group. The group had been struggling for
some time due to a lack of funding, but those who remained seemed determined to
bring the organization back to life. The organization was situated only a few blocks
from one of the city's major downtown high schools and had always offered an
outreach program for teenagers in the community. Recently there were eleven teens
on the roster, with three members listed as active, but the group had not met for
nearly three months. I was brought in to reorganize and breathe new life into the
youth group. I contacted the members listed on the roster, but at our first meeting
only one teenager attended. After three months, we had an active membership of
twenty-three, and we met twice a week. The group was fully engaged in conducting
community service projects and after-school personal growth and development ses-
sions. The difference was a needs assessment and a program designed around the
needs of the youths in the community.

A needs assessment can be formal and involve hiring professional consultants, or it
can be nothing more than sitting down and talking with those who are engaged in
the program. The kind of needs assessment you undertake will be dictated by
financial constraints, time constraints, and the regulations under which your school-
based organization functions. Regardless of your organization's dictates, you should
never attempt to organize a new program, group, or intervention without a needs
assessment and a formative evaluation.

Needs Assessment

Your needs assessment may rely on secondary data, such as census data or local
school and administrative reports. You may wish to hold public hearings or community forums where anyone may come and share their concerns. Your needs
assessment may also include surveys of the community, a focus group, or interviews with prospective participants in your program. A needs assessment does not

E. Clanton Harpine, *Group Interventions in Schools.*
© Springer Science+Business Media, LLC 2008

have to be complex to be effective. Sometimes the simplest procedures are the best. Your reason for conducting a needs assessment will to some extent determine the type of assessment that you require. If you are seeking funding, you will need a more detailed needs assessment, with statistical data to show whether your proposal is feasible and useful. If you are proposing a new group intervention in a school-based organization in which you already work, then possibly secondary data on similar programs or a simple survey of needs from prospective participants may suffice.

Before presenting your proposal for a new program or intervention, (1) review the checklist in Chapter 7, and make sure that your proposal meets the twenty-five requirements listed there; (2) if available, locate a model program or checklist of standards from state or national organizations affiliated with your school-based organization; and (3) if possible, consult with a recognized expert or peer who may be able to help you fine-tune your proposal.

A Formative Evaluation

Once you have approval, but before you begin to implement your group intervention program, decide how you will evaluate and measure the success of your program. I strongly suggest conducting a formative evaluation. Formative evaluations begin before your first group meeting.

The purpose of a formative evaluation is to guide and direct the program once it has been approved. Formative evaluations for group interventions are concerned with group process, communication difficulties, interaction, group cohesion, degree of trust in the group, self-disclosure, conflicts, and the number of participants voluntarily attending on a regular basis. A formative evaluation can help you guide and direct your group intervention, especially new interventions. Formative evaluations can help you fine-tune your program, and help you adjust and enhance the group intervention to meet the needs of the group with which you are working.

Your formative evaluation will most likely be descriptive in nature, describing what worked and what did not. Detailed documentation is essential. Field notes should include a detailed history from on-site observations, either by you or the group leader or from an outside observer. Participant observations and evaluations by members of the group are also essential in a formative evaluation. In-depth interviews or open-ended questionnaires can provide a wonderful inside look at the group. Providing anonymity on open-ended questionnaires can encourage participants who are reluctant to speak up during the group or to make often much-needed observations about how the group is functioning.

Formative evaluations should be conducted periodically; every three months is a comfortable time frame. With a new group, you may decide to include some means of formative evaluation on a regular ongoing basis. For example with the youth group mentioned at the beginning of the chapter, I included a weekly participant on-site observation report completed by myself as the group leader and a monthly participant open-ended evaluation completed by all group participants. This allowed me to continually receive anonymous feedback from the group members. They realized that they could make anonymous comments and suggestions on how the group was functioning without retribution from other group members. As the group developed, we were able to discuss some of these comments and suggestions and thereby help the group grow into a much stronger community-based program.

I like to use written, open-ended questionnaires because they give me a written record for program evaluation without having to tape interviews or group sessions. Qualitative data are essential in effective formative program evaluation. Open-ended questionnaires allow group participants to express their opinions and feelings in a much less-restrained manner than Likert-scale questionnaires, which tend to force comments and responses into a quantitatively measured pattern.

If possible, I suggest using both qualitative and quantitative measures in your evaluations. Qualitative measures include open-ended questionnaires, interviews, surveys, observations, field notes, use of existing data or statistics, comparative groups, or other descriptive forms of data collection. Quantitative measures follow the dictates of experimental design, and allow you to statistically analyze and make comparisons to other populations. If you are not familiar with qualitative or quantitative data collection, seek additional help from peers or experts who have completed studies using both techniques.

For program evaluation, I like to gather as much unrestrained information as possible from group members. Open-ended questionnaires aid in this process. I often incorporate more traditional data gathering, as well. For example, with the youth group mentioned above, I also collected standard Likert-type scales on cohesion and health risk behaviors. Using both qualitative and quantitative data gathering strengthens your formative evaluation.

This is especially true with group-centered interventions, because the idea behind a group-centered intervention is to use group process to bring about change. Continuous, ongoing formative evaluation is the best way to ensure using group process and group cohesion to accomplish the desired change. Your goals in a formative evaluation should always be (1) to answer key questions that you outlined in your initial needs assessment, and (2) to evaluate the original goals for implementing the group intervention.

Process Evaluation

Formative evaluations are conducted while the intervention is in process. Process evaluations are conducted at the close of a program or group intervention or, if the group is to be ongoing, at a designated, defined point of evaluation.

Every program or intervention should include a process evaluation, which provides detailed documentation on how the intervention was conducted and what the program accomplished. Data should be gathered from the planning stages until the conclusion of the program. Field notes, on-site observations, participant observations, in-depth interviews, open-ended questionnaires, and any other data gathered from the group should be kept in written or transcript form.

To enhance quality control of the data gathered, try to use more than one type of data-gathering process. For example, in the previously mentioned group I kept extensive field notes from the very first meeting with the organization and from every meeting with members of the organization. I conducted a case study using weekly participant-leader observations and monthly open-ended participant evaluations that included written transcripts from the participants.

Because I needed more exact statistical evidence of outcome or benefits from the group for my financial backers, I also included quantitative data collection: questionnaires, surveys, pre-and posttesting, and comparison to a control group. My quantitative measures showed long-term attitude and behavioral change. My qualitative, open-ended, observational measures showed which group intervention techniques had been most effective and what the response had been from the group participants.

A process evaluation should describe your program so completely, including quantitative and qualitative evaluative measures, that others may replicate your group intervention from your evaluation report. Detailed documentation is essential. To enhance quality control, measure the formative development of the group and the long-term endurance of the group. Rely on more than one data source. If possible, use both quantitative and qualitative measures. Evaluate problems in the formative stages by asking: What can we do to change or alleviate this problem? Involving group participants in the evaluation will enhance member involvement. For the outcome process evaluation, again ask: What could we have done differently to change or make this group function more effectively? Also remember to list in the formative and process evaluative stages the advantages or successes that your group intervention program experienced. Try to have both descriptive and statistical evidence to support your lists of successful accomplishments, especially if the continuation of your program is determined by financial backers or administrative approval from the school-based organization within which you work.

Outcome Evaluation

If the funding or administrative agency is primarily concerned with the results or effect of your group intervention, an outcome evaluation may be what is needed. An outcome group research design should incorporate reliable and valid measurement, introduction of a new group intervention, and an evaluation of the outcome of that intervention.

Experimental Design

The best form of outcome evaluation is an experimental design that incorporates (1) randomized selection of participants; (2) valid measurement of pre- and postintervention; (3) a large number of participants who are randomly assigned to the group intervention (treatment group), to no intervention (control group), or to a comparison group; (4) a group intervention or treatment that can be reliably introduced and measured; and (5) statistical evaluation that meets the constraints of scientific study (Royse, Thyer, Padgett, & Logan, 2006). Unfortunately, in program evaluation, true scientific study is not always possible (Rappaport & Seidman, 2000).

Quasi-Experimental Design

When it is not possible to follow the guidelines of a true experimental study, you may choose a quasi-experimental methodology. Quasi-experimental designs may make comparisons to another group when you cannot randomly select students to participate in your intervention. In our opening example, everyone at the youth center was included in the study. We could not randomly select a treatment group; therefore, for comparison it was necessary to use a comparable group at another youth facility.

A quasi-experimental methodology may fit your school-based evaluation needs. One caution: a quasi-experimental evaluation cannot provide conclusive evidence that a group intervention worked, was responsible for an observed change, or is better than an alternative program, for quasi-experimental studies do not use randomized samples and often do not include a control group.

Let us return to our above example of the youth group. If we are organizing a new drug prevention program through a community-based organization, which works with teens after school to help teens prevent or reduce health risk behaviors, such as alcohol, smoking, premarital sex, and substance abuse, then it may be impossible to set up a true scientific experiment. We may not have a sufficient number of participants involved to randomly assign them to a treatment group and a control group. The community-based organization may wish for all members to participate in the designed group intervention. This is often the case, which leaves no group for comparative evaluation or outcome research. Therefore, it may be necessary to locate a control group from another similar community-based organization or school. This allows comparison, but not randomization. Also, the ideal posttest for scientific effectiveness of the drug program might be random urine sample testing, but once again, the community-based organization might refuse permission to conduct random urine testing, fearing that it would reduce the number of teens attending their program. Therefore, an outcome evaluator might have to settle for a pencil-and-paper measure of attitudes toward drugs or self-report of recent drug use. At this point, it is also essential to remember that all teens in our evaluation must freely volunteer to participate in the study and in the outcome evaluation, and their confidentiality must be scrupulously respected.

So, if you are planning to conduct an outcome evaluation of your group intervention, you must plan the evaluation procedures to be followed before you begin the group intervention. You cannot undertake an outcome evaluation to gather scientific evidence that supports the effectiveness of your group intervention after the program has ended, unless you have laid the groundwork for an outcome evaluation before implementation.

If you are not familiar with conducting experimental or quasi-experimental studies, I strongly suggest that you team with an experienced researcher or engage in an extensive study of research methods before undertaking such a project. Research methods courses are offered at universities, and the market offers numerous textbooks. One book that I highly recommend for program evaluators is *Program Evaluation: An Introduction, 4th ed.* by Royse, Thyer, Padgett, and Logan (2006). This easy-to-read book specifically talks about program evaluation. There are also many fine books that can guide you through experimental research and statistical analysis.

The goals or aims of your organization and the objectives of your group intervention will help you determine which outcome measures are suitable for your project. Your design should follow the research question, hypothesis, or purpose of the evaluation: What are you trying to accomplish or prove? Your objective as a program evaluator should be to find the outcome evaluation design that provides the most credible information that it is possible to obtain in your school-based group situation.

The Written Report

Begin the report with a one-page executive summary or brief report. Then state the goals and objectives of the project. Describe the program in detail, and give a detailed background description of the intervention and evaluation undertaken. Explain the methodology for the evaluation, sampling techniques, data collection, analysis, and strategies for quality control.

In the results section, present the themes that emerged from analysis and interpretation of the data and include case studies of events that happened in the group or explain how individual participants were influenced by the group intervention. Graphic presentations of findings are frequently helpful with funding agencies. Your conclusions and recommendations should be concise and linked directly to the data gathered, include limitations and strengths of the study, and incorporate comparison to similar programs.

Real-World Applications

Observational Extensions

Select a group that you would like to observe or work with. Conduct an hour-long observation using the following group observation form:

Observation Form

Day of Observation:

Starting Time:

Ending Time:

Name of Group:

Brief Description of Group:

Overall Purpose of Group:

What is the specific purpose of the group meeting or gathering that you are observing?

Have you observed this group before? When?

What do you hope to learn from this observation?

Observation:

Observe what is happening in your group.

Effort:

Persistence:

Facial Expressions:

Bodily Gestures:

Analysis of Group Needs:

What does the group need from the participants in order to continue?

Does the group have a set criteria or goal(s)? Do the members follow their criteria or announced goals? Give examples.

Motivations Observed:

What type of motivating strategies were used in the group during the observation? Be specific.

Were the motivating strategies successful? Why or why not?

Were there problems associated with the motivating strategies used in your group? Explain.

Group Member Participation:

Did group members work well together? Why or why not?

Did group members come to the session with preconceived expectations?

Give examples from the observation.

Did anyone block or prevent work of the group?

How did the group leader keep the group on task?

Were participants free to speak their opinions or was participation stifled?

Was such an atmosphere helpful or harmful to the group?

Proposal for Change:

In your opinion, was the group successful? Why?

If you were brought in to change this group and help this group function more successfully, what would you propose?

What do you suggest? Why?

How would your proposal be implemented?

Why would your proposal be better than the present system?

What would be the expected response from the group to your proposal?

(Remember to look back at Chapter 7 to the checklist of twenty-five rules and questions.)

References

Ablon, J., & Jones, E. (2002). Validity of controlled clinical trials of psychotherapy: Findings from the NIMH treatment of depression collaborative research program. *American Journal of Psychiatry, 159*, 775–783.

Abrams, D., Rutland, A., & Cameron, L. (2003). The development of subjective group dynamics: Children's judgments of normative and deviant in-group and out-group individuals. *Child Development, 74*, 1840–1856.

Adelman, H. S., & Taylor, L. (2006). Mental health in schools and public health. *Public Health Report, 121*, 294–298.

Arrow, H. (2005). Chaos, complexity, and catastrophe: The nonlinear dynamics perspective. In S. A. Wheelan, (Ed.), *The handbook of group research and practice*. Thousand Oaks, CA: Sage.

Association for Specialists in Group Work. (2000). Professional standards for the training of group workers. *Group Worker, 29*, 1–10.

Axline, V. M. (1955). Play therapy procedures and results. *American Journal of Orthopsychiatry, 25*, 618–626.

Baker, L. M., Dreher, J., & Guthrie, J. T. (Eds.). (2000). *Engaging young readers: Promoting achievement and motivation*. New York: Guilford Press.

Bandura, A. (1977). Self-efficacy: Toward a unifying theory of behavioral change. *Psychological Review, 84*, 191–215.

Bandara, A. (1986). *Social foundations of thought and action: A social cognitive theory.* Englewood Cliffs, NJ: Prentice-Hall.

Bandura, A. (1995). Exercise of personal and collective efficacy in changing societies. In A. Bandura (Ed.), *Self-efficacy in changing societies* (pp. 1–45). New York: Cambridge University Press.

Bandura, A. (1997). *Self-efficacy: The exercise of control*. New York: W. H. Freeman.

Bandura, A., Barbaranelli, C., Vittorio Caprara, G., & Pastorelli, C. (2001). Self-efficacy beliefs as shapers of children's aspirations and career trajectories. *Child Development, 72*, 187–206.

Bandura, A., & Cervone, D. (2000). Self-evaluative and self-efficacy mechanisms governing the motivational effects of goal systems. In E. T. Higgins & A. W. Kruglanski (Eds.), *Motivational science: Social and personality perspectives* (pp. 202–214). Philadelphia: Psychology Press.

Barber, B., Eccles, J., & Stone, M. (2001). Whatever happened to the jock, the brain, and the princess? Youth adult pathways linked to adolescent activity involvement and social identity. *Journal of Adolescent Research, 16*, 429–455.

Baumeister, R. F., & Leary, M. R. (1995). The need to belong: Desire for interpersonal attachments as a fundamental human motivation. *Psychological Review, 103*, 5–33.

Benware, C., & Deci, E. L. (1984). The quality of learning with an active versus passive motivational set. *American Educational Research Journal, 21*, 755–765.

Black, M. M., & Krishnakumar, A. (1998). Children in low-income, urban settings: Interventions to promote mental health and well-being. *American Psychologist, 53*, 635–646.

Bluestone, J. (1999). School-based peer therapy to facilitate mourning in latency-age children following sudden parental death: Cases of Joan, age 10½, and Roberta age 9 ½, with follow-up 8 years later. In N. Boyd Webb (Ed.), *Play therapy with children in crisis: Individual, group, and family treatment* (2ⁿᵈ ed.) (pp. 225–251). New York: Guilford Press.

Blundon, J. A., & Schaefer, C. E. (2006). The use of group play therapy for children with social skills deficits. In H. Gerard Kaduson and C. E. Schaefer (Eds.), *Short-term play therapy for children* (2ⁿᵈ ed.) (pp. 336–375). New York: Guilford Press.

Boyd Webb, N. (1999). *Playtherapy with children in crisis: Individual, group, and family treatment* (2ⁿᵈ ed.). New York: Guilford Press.

Brooks-Gunn, J. (2003). Do you believe in magic? What we can expect from early childhood intervention programs. *Social Policy Report: Giving Child and Youth Development Knowledge Away, 17*, 3–14.

Buhs, E. S., Ladd, G. W., & Herald, S. (2006). Peer exclusion and victimization: Processes that mediate the relation between peer group rejection and children's classroom engagement and achievement? *Journal of Educational Psychology, 98*, 1–13.

Burlingame, G. M., Fuhriman, A. J., & Johnson, J. (2004). Processes and outcomes in group counseling and psychotherapy: A perspective. In J. L. Delucia-Waack, D. Gerrity, C. R. Kalodner, & M. T. Riva (Eds.), *Handbook of counseling and psychotherapy* (pp. 49–61). Thousand Oaks, CA: Sage.

Carmichael, K. (1991). Play therapy: Role in reading improvement. *Reading Improvement, 28*, 273–276.

Catalano, R. F., Mazza, J. J., Harachi, T. W., Abbott, R. D., Haggerty, K. P., & Fleming, C. B. (2003). Raising healthy children through enhancing social development in elementary school: Results after 1.5 years. *Journal of School Psychology, 41*, 143–164.

Christenson, T. M. (2006). A group for children who have been abused. In M. Schneider Corey and G. Corey (Eds.), *Groups: Process and practice* (7ᵗʰ ed.) (pp. 314–319). Belmont, CA: Thomson Brooks/Cole.

Clanton Harpine, E. (2005). After-school community-based prevention project. Paper presented at the annual convention of the American Psychological Association, Washington, DC, August.

Clanton Harpine, E. (2006). Developing an effective cost-efficient after-school prevention program for community-based organizations. Paper presented at the annual convention of the American Psychological Association, Washington, DC, August.

Clanton Harpine, E. (2007a). A community-based after-school prevention program: a one year review of the Camp Sharigan program. Paper presented at the annual convention of the American Psychological Association, Washington, DC, August.

Clanton Harpine, E. (2007b). *Erasing failure in the classroom: Camp Sharigan, a ready-to-use motivational reading program for grades 1–3.* Aiken, SC: The Camp Sharigan Project.

Clanton Harpine, E., & Reid, T. (2008a). *An after-school group-centered intervention for children labeled at-risk of failing.* Manuscript submitted for publication.

Clanton Harpine, E., & Reid, T. (2008b). *Preventing school failure in Hispanic immigrant communities: A group-centered intervention.* Manuscript submitted for publication.

Connell, J. P., & Ryan, R. M. (1985). A developmental theory of motivation in the classroom. *Teacher Education Quarterly, 11*, 64–77.

Damasio, A. R. (1994). *Descartes' error: Emotion, reason, and the human brain.* New York: Putnam.

Deci, E. L., Nezlek, J., & Sheinman, L. (1981). Characteristics of the rewarder and intrinsic motivation of the rewardee. *Journal of Personality and Social Psychology, 40*, 1–10.

Deci, E. L., & Ryan, R. M. (1985). *Intrinsic motivation and self-determination in human behavior.* New York: Plenum.

Deci, E. L., Ryan, R. M., & Williams, G. C. (1995). Need satisfaction and the self-regulation of learning. *Learning and Individual Differences, 8*, 165–183.

Deci, E., Vallerand, R., Pelletier, L., & Ryan, R. (1991). Motivation and education: The self-determination perspective. *Educational Psychologist, 26*, 325–347.

Dishion, T. J., Capaldi, D. M., & Yoerger, K. (1999). Middle childhood antecedents to progressions in male adolescent substance use: An ecological analysis of risk and protection. *Journal of Adolescent Research, 14*, 175–205.

Dishion, T. J., McCord, J., & Poulin, F. (1999). When interventions harm: Peer groups and problem behavior. *American Psychologist, 54,* 755–764.

Donnelly, J., Duncan, D. F., Goldfarb, E., & Eadie, C. (1999). Sexuality attitudes and behaviors of self-described very religious urban students in middle school. *Psychological Reports, 85,* 607–610.

Donoghue, A. R., Wheeler, A. R., Prout, M. F., Wilson, H. W., & Reinecke, M. A. (2006). Understanding depression in children and adolescents: Cognitive-behavioral interventions. In R. B. Mennuti, A. Freeman, & R. W. Christner (Eds.), *Cognitive-behavioral interventions in educational settings: A handbook for practice* (pp. 121–138). New York: Routledge.

Duckworth, A. L., Peterson, C., Matthews, M. D., & Kelly, D. R. (2007). Grit: Perseverance and passion for long-term goals. *Journal of Personality and Social Psychology, 92, 1087–1101.*

DuPaul, G. J., Vile Junod, R. E., & Flammer, L. M. (2006). Attention-deficit/hyperactivity disorder. In R. B. Mennuti, A. Freeman, & R. W. Christner (Eds.), *Cognitive-behavioral interventions in educational settings: A handbook for practice* (pp. 139–161). New York: Routledge.

Dweck, C. (2000). *Self-theories: Their role in motivation, personality, and development.* Philadelphia: Psychology Press.

Eccles, J. S., & Barber, B. L. (1999). Student council, volunteering, basketball, or marching band: What kind of extracurricular involvement matters? *Journal of Adolescent Research, 14,* 10–43.

Elliot, A. J., & Dweck, C. S. (2005). *Handbook of competence and motivation.* New York: Guilford Press.

Fall, M. (1999). A play therapy intervention and its relationship to self-efficacy and learning behaviors. *Professional School Counseling, 2,* 194–205.

Fawson, P. C., & Moore, S. A. (1999). Reading incentive programs: Beliefs and practices. *Reading Psychology, 20,* 325–340.

Finn, J. D., Gerber, S. B., & Boyd-Zaharias, J. (2005). Small classes in the early grades, academic achievement, and graduating from high school. *Journal of Educational Psychology, 97,* 214–223.

Fischhoff, B., Parker, A., DeBruin, W. B., Downs, J., Palmgren, C., Dawes, R., & Manski, C. (2000). Teen expectations for significant life events. *Public Opinion Quarterly, 64,* 189–205.

Flammer, A. (1995). Developmental analysis of control beliefs. In A. Bandura (Ed.), *Self-efficacy in changing societies* (pp. 69–113). New York: Cambridge University Press.

Fleming, C. B., Harachi, T. W., Cortes, R. C., Abbott, R. D., & Catalano, R. F. (2004). Level and change in reading scores and attention problems during elementary school as predictors of problem behavior in middle school. *Journal of Emotional and Behavioral Disorders, 12,* 130–144.

Frank, L. K. (1955). Play in personality development. *American Journal of Orthopsychiatry, 25,* 576–590.

Frankl, V. (1969). *The will to meaning.* Cleveland: World Publishing.

Fuhriman, A., & Burlingame, G. M. (1990). Consistency of matter: A comparative analysis of individual and group process variables. *The Counseling Psychologist, 18,* 6–63.

Fuhriman, A., & Burlingame, G. M. (1994). *Handbook of group psychotherapy: An empirical and clinical synthesis.* New York: John Wiley & Sons.

Garai, J. (2001). A humanistic approach to art therapy. In J. Rubin (Ed.), *Approaches to art therapy* (pp. 188–207). New York: Brunner-Routledge.

Gazda, G. M. (1989). *Group counseling: A developmental approach* (4th ed.). Boston: Allyn and Bacon.

George, L. K., Larson, D. B., Koenig, H. G., & McCullough, M. E. (2000). Spirituality and health: What we know, what we need to know. *Journal of Social and Clinical Psychology, 19,* 102–116.

Gerard Kaduson, H., & Schaefer, C. E. (2006). *Short-term play therapy for children* (2nd ed). New York: Guilford Press.

Gladding, S., & Newsome, D. (2003). Art in counseling. In C. Malchiodi (Ed.), *Handbook of art therapy* (pp. 243–253). New York: Guilford Press.

Gosch, E. A., & Flannery-Schroeder, E. (2006). School-based interventions for anxiety disorders. In R. B. Mennuti, A. Freeman, & R. W. Christner (Eds.), *Cognitive-behavioral interventions in educational settings: A handbook for practice* (pp. 66–88). New York: Routledge.

Grawitch, M., David, C., Munz, & Kramer, T. J. (2003). Effects of member mood states on creative performance in temporary workgroups. *Group Dynamics: Theory, Research and Practice, 7*, 41–54.

Greenberg, M., Domitrovich, C., & Bumbarger, B. (2001). The prevention of mental disorders in school-aged children: Current state of the field. *Prevention and Treatment, 4*, Article 0001a. Retrieved May 9, 2005, from http://journals.apa.org/prevention/volume 4/pre0040001a.html.

Greenberg, M., Weissberg, R. P., O'Brien, M. U., Zins, J. E., Fredricks, L., Resnick, H., & Elias, M. J. (2003). Enhancing school-based prevention and youth development through coordinated social, emotional, and academic learning. *American Psychologist, 58*, 466–474.

Greene, J. P., & Winters, M. (2006). *Leaving boys behind: Public high school graduation rates.* New York: Manhattan Institute for Policy Research.

Hawkins, J. D., Catalano, R. F., Kosterman, R., Abbott, R., & Hill, K. G. (1999). Preventing adolescent health-risk behaviors by strengthening protection during childhood. *Archives of Pediatrics and Adolescent Medicine, 153*, 226–234.

Hawkins, J. D., Herrenkohl, T., Farrington, D. P., Brewer, D., Catalano, R. F., & Harachi, T. W. (1998). A review of predictors of youth violence. In R. Loeber & D. P. Farrington (Eds.), *Serious and violent juvenile offenders: Risk factors and successful interventions* (pp. 106–146). Thousand Oaks, CA: Sage.

Hellendoorn, J., Van der Kooij, R., & Sutton-Smith, B. (Eds.). (1994). *Play and intervention.* New York: State University of New York Press.

Henderlong, J., & Lepper, M. R. (2002). The effects of praise on children's intrinsic motivation: A review and synthesis. *Psychological Bulletin, 128*, 774–795.

Hoag, M. A., & Burlingame, G. M. (1997). Evaluating the effectiveness of child and adolescent group treatment: A meta-analytic review. *Journal of Clinical Child Psychology, 26, 234–246.*

Hogg, M. A., Abrams, D., Otten, S., & Hinkle, S. (2004). The social identity perspective: Intergroup relations, self-conception, and small groups. *Small Group Research, 35*, 246–276.

Holmes, S. E., & Kivlighan, D. M. (2000). Comparison of therapeutic factors in group and individual treatment processes. *Journal of Counseling Psychology, 47*, 478–484.

Holtz, R. (2004). Group cohesion, attitude projection, and opinion certainty: Beyond interaction. *Group Dynamics: Theory, Research, and Practice, 8*, 112–125.

Huebner, A., & Mancini, J. (2003). Shaping structured out-of-school time use among youth: The effects of self, family, and friend systems. *Journal of Youth and Adolescence, 32*, 453–463.

Jacobs, E., & Schimmel, C. (2005). Small group counseling. In C. A. Sink (Ed.) *Contemporary school counseling: Theory, research, and practice* (pp. 82–115). New York: Lahaska Press.

Johnson, J. E., Pulsipher, D., Ferrin, S. L., Burlingame, G. M., Davies, D. R., & Gleave, R. (2006). Measuring group processes: A comparison of the GCQ and CCI. *Group Dynamics: Theory, Research, and Practice, 10*, 136–145.

Kearney, C. A., Lemos, A., & Silverman, J. (2006). School refusal behavior. In R. B. Mennuti, A. Freeman, & R. W. Christner (Eds.), *Cognitive-behavioral interventions in educational settings: A handbook for practice* (pp. 89–105). New York: Routledge.

Kernis, M. H. (2003). Toward a conceptualization of optimal self-esteem. *Psychological Inquiry, 14*, 1–26.

Koestner, R., Ryan, R. M., Bernieri, F., & Holt, K. (1984). Setting limits on children's behavior: The differential effects of controlling versus informational styles on intrinsic motivation and creativity. *Journal of Personality, 52*, 233–248.

Kram Laudenslager, K. (2006). A group for elementary school children of divorce and changing families. In M. Schneider Corey and G. Corey (Eds.), *Groups: Process and practice* (7th ed.) (pp. 305–309). Belmont, CA: Thomson Brooks/Cole.

Kulic, K. R., Dagley, J. C., & Horne, A. M. (2001). Prevention groups with children and adolescents. *Journal for Specialists in Group Work, 26*, 211–218.

Kulic, K. R., Horne, A. M., & Dagley, J. C. (2004). A comprehensive review of prevention groups for children and adolescents. *Group Dynamics: Theory, Research, and Practice, 8*, 139–151.

Landreth, G. L. (1991). *Play therapy: The art of the relationship.* Muncie, IN: Accelerated Development.

Landreth, G. L. (2002). *Play therapy: The art of the relationship.* New York: Brunner-Routledge.

Lebo, D. (1955). The development of play as a form of therapy. *American Journal of Psychiatry, 12*, 418–442.

Lepper, M. R., & Greene, D. (1975). Turning play into work: Effects of adult surveillance and extrinsic rewards on children's intrinsic motivation. *Journal of Personality and Social Psychology, 31*, 479–486.

Levy, R. B. (1972). *Self-revelation through relationships*. Englewood Cliffs, NJ: Prentice-Hall.

Luft, J. (1984). *Group processes: An introduction to group dynamics*. Palo Alto, CA: Mayfield.

Lyon, G. R. (April 28, 1988). Overview of reading and literacy initiatives. Testimony before the Committee on Labor and Human Resources, Senate Dirkson Building. Retrieved November 27, 2006, from http://www.cdl.org/resource-library/pdf/lyon_testimonies.pdf.

Magen, R. H., & Mangiardi, E. (2005). Groups and individual change. In S. A. Wheelan (Ed.), *The Handbook of Group Research and Practice* (pp. 351–361). Thousand Oaks, CA: Sage.

Mahoney, J. L. (2000). School extracurricular activity participation as a moderator in the development of antisocial patterns. *Child Development, 71*, 502–516.

Mahoney, J. L., & Stattin, H. (2000). Leisure activities and adolescent antisocial behavior: The role of structure and social context. *Journal of Adolescence, 23*, 113–127.

Malchiodi, C. A. (2005). *Expressive therapies*. New York: Guilford Press.

Marmarosh, C., Holtz, A., & Schottenbauer, M. (2005). Group cohesiveness, group-derived collective self-esteem, group-derived hope, and the well-being of group therapy members. *Group Dynamics: Theory Research and Practice, 9*, 32–44.

Marmarosh, C., & Markin, R. D. (2007). Group and personal attachments: Two is better than one when predicting college adjustment. *Group Dynamics: Theory Research and Practice, 11*, 153–164.

Mennuti, R. B., Freeman, A., & Christner, R. W. (Eds.). (2006). *Cognitive-behavioral interventions in educational settings: A handbook for practice*. New York: Routledge.

Miech, R. A., Eaton, W. W., & Brennan, K. (2005). Mental health disparities across education and sex: A prospective analysis examining how they persist over the life course. *Journals of Gerontology, 60B*, 93–98.

Miller, R. L., & Shinn, M. (2005). Learning from communities: Overcoming difficulties in the dissemination of prevention and promotion efforts. *American Journal of Community Psychology, 35*, 169–183.

Morris, D., Shaw, B., & Perney, J. (1990). Helping low readers in grades 2 and 3: An after-school volunteer tutoring program. *Elementary School Journal, 91*, 133–150.

Multon, K. D., Brown, S. D., & Lent, R. W. (1991). Relation of self-efficacy beliefs to academic outcomes: A meta-analytic investigation. *Journal of Counseling Psychology, 18*, 30–38.

Nastasi, B. K., Moore, R. B., & Varjas, K. M. (2004). *School-based mental health services: Creating comprehensive and culturally specific programs*. Washington, DC: American Psychological Association.

National Reading Panel. (2000). *Teaching children to read: An evidence-based assessment of the scientific research literature on reading and its implications for reading instruction* (NIH Publication No. 00-4754). Washington, DC: National Institute for Literacy.

Nazroo, J. Y. (2003). The structuring of ethnic inequalities in health: Economic position, racial discrimination, racism. *American Journal of Public Health, 93*, 277–234.

Nelson, G., Prilleltensky, I., & Peters, R. (2003). Mental Health promotion and the prevention of mental health problems in the community. In P. Firestone and W. Marshall (Eds.), *Abnormal psychology: perspectives* (2nd ed.) (pp. 462–479). Scarborough, Ontario, Canada: Prentice-Hall.

Nelson, G., Westhues, A., & MacLeod, J. (2003). A meta-analysis of longitudinal research on preschool prevention programs for children. *Prevention and Treatment, 6*, Article 0031a. Retrieved May 9, 2005, from http://journals.apa.org/prevention/volume 6/preoo60031a.html.

Noam, G. C., & Hermann, C. A. (2002). Where education and mental health meet: Developmental prevention and early intervention in schools. *Developmental Psychopathology, 14*, 861–875.

Obiakor, F. E. (2001). *It even happens in "good" schools: Responding to cultural diversity in today's classrooms*. Thousand Oaks, CA: Sage.

Ogrodniczuk, J. S., & Piper, W. E. (2003). The effect of group climate on outcome in two forms of short-term group therapy. *Group Dynamics: Theory Research and Practice, 7*, 64–76.

Oldfather, P. (2002). Introduction: Overcoming motivation problems in literacy learning: Part 1 of 2. *Reading and Writing Quarterly, 18*, 201–203.

Orfield, G., & Lee, C. (2005). Why segregation matters: Poverty and educational inequality. Cambridge, MA: The Civil Right Project at Harvard University.

Parsons, R. D. (2006). *Counseling strategies that work! Evidence-based interventions for school counselors.* New York: Pearson.

Petraitis, J., Flay, B., & Miller, T. Q. (1995). Reviewing theories of adolescent substance abuse. *Psychological Bulletin, 117*, 67–86.

Pintrich, P. R., & Schunk, D. H. (2002). Motivation in education: Theory, research, and applications (2nd ed.). Englewood Cliffs, NJ: Prentice Hall.

Piper, W. E., Ogrodniczuk, J. S., Lamarche, C., Hilscher, T., & Joyce, A. S. (2005). Level of alliance, pattern of alliance, and outcomes in short-term group therapy. *International Journal of Group Psychotherapy, 55*, 527–550.

Pressley, M., Mohan, L., Raphael, L. M., & Fingeret, L. (2007). How does Bennett Woods Elementary School produce such high reading and writing achievement? *Journal of Educational Psychology, 99*, 221–240.

Prilleltensky, I., Nelson, G., & Pierson, L. (2001). The role of power and control in children's lives: An ecological analysis of pathways toward wellness, resilience and problems. *Journal of Community and Applied Social Psychology, 11*, 143–158.

Pumfrey, P., & Elliott, C. (1970). Play therapy, social adjustment and reading attainment. *Educational Research, 12*, 183–193.

Randolph, K. A., Fraser, M. W., & Orthner, D. K. (2004). Educational resilience among youth at risk. *Substance Use & Misuse 39*, 747–767.

Rappaport, J., & Seidman, E. (Eds.) (2000). *Handbook of community psychology.* New York: Kluwer Academic Plenum Publishers.

Ray, D., Bratton, S., Rhine, T., & Jones, L. (2001). The effectiveness of play therapy: Responding to the critics. *International Journal of Play Therapy, 10*, 85–108.

Reeve, J. (1993). The face of interest. *Motivation and Emotion, 17*, 353–375.

Rigby, C. S., Deci, E. L., Patrick, B. C., & Ryan, R. M. (1992). Beyond the intrinsic-extrinsic dichotomy: Self-determination in motivation and learning. *Motivation and Emotion, 16*, 165–185.

Riviere, S. (2006). Short-term play therapy for children with disruptive behavior disorders. In H. Gerard Kaduson & C. E. Schaefer (Eds.), *Short-term play therapy for children* (2nd ed.) (pp. 51–70). New York: Guilford Press.

Rogers, C. (1951). *Client-centered therapy: Its current practice, implications, and theory.* Boston: Houghton Mifflin.

Rogers, C. (1969). *Freedom to learn.* Columbus, OH: Merrill.

Rogers, C. (1976). The process of the basic encounter group. In J. A. DeVito (Ed.), *Communication: Concepts and processes,* (2nd ed.) (pp. 149–172). Englewood Cliffs, NJ: Prentice-Hall.

Royse, D., Thyer, B. A., Padgett, D. K., & Logan, T. K. (2006). *Program Evaluation: An Introduction* (4th ed.). Belmont, CA: Thomson Brooks/Cole.

Ryan, R. M., & Deci, E. L. (2000). Intrinsic and extrinsic motivations: Classic definitions and new directions. *Contemporary Educational Psychology, 25*, 54–67.

Sandler, I., Ostrom, A., Bitner, M. J. Ayers, T. S., Wolchik, S., & Daniels, V. S. (2005). Developing effective prevention services for the real world: A prevention service development model. *American Journal of Community Psychology, 35*, 127–142.

Schneider Corey, M., & Corey, G. (2006). *Groups: Process and practice* (7th ed.). Belmont, CA: Thomson Brooks/Cole.

Schunk, D. H. (1989). Self-efficacy and achievement behaviors. *Educational Psychology Review, 1*, 173–208.

Schunk, D. H., & Pajares, F. (2005). Competence perceptions and academic functioning. In A. J. Elliot & C. S. Dweck (Eds.), *Handbook of competence and motivation* (pp. 85–104). New York: Guilford Press.

Schunk, D. M. (1991). Self-efficacy and academic motivation. *Educational Psychologist, 26*, 233–262.

Schunk, D. M. (1995). Self-efficacy and education and instruction. In J. E. Maddux (Ed.), *Self-efficacy, adaptation, and adjustment: Theory, research, and application* (pp. 281–303). New York: Plenum Press.

Schwarzer, R., & Fuchs, R. (1995). Changing risk behaviors and adopting health behaviors: The role of self-efficacy beliefs. In A. Bandura (Ed.), *Self-efficacy in changing societies* (pp. 259–288). New York: Cambridge University Press.

Segal, N. L. (1999). *Entwined lives: Twins and what they tell us about human behavior.* New York: Plume.

Seligman, M. E. P. (1990). *Learned optimism.* New York: Simon & Schuster.

Shechtman, Z., & Gluk, O. (2005). An investigation of therapeutic factors in children's groups. *Group Dynamics: Theory, Research, and Practice, 9,* 127–134.

Shechtman, Z., & Katz, E. (2007). Therapeutic bonding in group as an explanatory variable of progress in the social competence of students with learning disabilities. *Group Dynamics: Theory, Research, and Practice, 11,* 117–128.

Shechtman, Z., & Rybko, J. (2004). Attachment style and observed initial self-disclosure as explanatory variables of group functioning. *Group Dynamics: Theory, Research, and Practice, 8,* 207–220.

Sink, C. A. (2005). *Contemporary school counseling: Theory, research, and practice.* New York: Lahaska Press.

Slavin, R. E., & Madden, N. A. (2001). *Success for all: Research and reform in elementary education.* Mahwah, NY: Lawrence Erlbaum.

Slavin, R. L. (2002). Operative group dynamics in school settings: Structuring to enhance educational, social, and emotional progress. *Group 26,* 297–308.

Snowden, L. R. (2005). Racial, cultural and ethnic disparities in health and mental health: Toward theory and research at community levels. *American Journal of Community Psychology, 35,* 1–8.

Steiner, H. (Ed.). (2004). *Handbook of mental health interventions in children and adolescents: An integrated developmental approach.* San Francisco: Jossey-Bass.

Sternberg, R. J. (2000). *Handbook of intelligence.* New York: Cambridge University Press.

Swann, W. B., & Pittman, T. S. (1977). Initiating play activity of children: The moderating influence of verbal cues on intrinsic motivation. *Child Development 48,* 1128–1132.

Thorkildsen, T. A. (2002). Literacy as a lifestyle: Negotiating the curriculum to facilitate motivation. *Reading and Writing Quarterly, 18,* 321–328.

Twenge, J., & Campbell, W. K. (2002). Self-esteem and socioeconomic status: A meta-analytic review. *Personality and Social Psychology Review, 6,* 59–71.

Underwood, L. G., & Teresi, J. A. (2002). The daily spiritual experience and scale: Development, theoretical description, reliability, exploratory factor analysis, and preliminary construct validity using health-related data. *Annals of Behavioral Medicine, 24,* 22–33.

Weinstein, R. S. (2006). Overcoming inequality in schooling: A call to action from community psychology. *American Journal of Community Psychology, 30,* 21–42.

Weissberg, R., Kumpfer, K., & Seligman, M. (2003). Prevention that works for children and youth: An introduction. *American Psychologist, 58,* 425–432.

Wentzel, K. R. (2003). School adjustment. In W. Reynolds & G. Miller (Eds.), *Handbook of psychology: Vol. 7. Educational psychology* (pp. 235–258). New York: Wiley.

Wheelan, S. A. (2005). *The handbook of group research and practice.* Thousand Oaks, CA: Sage.

Yalom, I. D., & Leszcz, M. (2005). *The theory and practice of group psychotherapy* (5th ed.). New York: Basic Books.

Zimmerman, B. J. (1995). Self-efficacy and educational development. In A. Bandura (Ed.), *Self-efficacy in changing societies* (pp. 202–231). New York: Cambridge University Press.

Zimmerman, B. J., & Martinez-Pons, M. (1988). Construct validation of a strategy model of student self-regulated learning. *Journal of Educational Psychology 80,* 284–290.

Index

LaVergne, TN USA
07 December 2009
166095LV00002B/115/P

9 780387 773155